THE GOLDEN CALM

THE GOLDEN CALM

An English Lady's Life in Moghul Delhi

Reminiscences by Emily, Lady Clive Bayley,
and by her father, Sir Thomas Metcalfe

Edited by
M.M. KAYE

Webb&Bower
EXETER, ENGLAND

Frontispiece: Emily Metcalfe shortly after arrival in India in 1848

Front and Back End-papers:
Each end-paper shows a different form of the Style and Titles by which the Emperor Bahadur Shah addressed the Agent of the Governor General attached to His Majesty's Court.

Publisher's Note

The main text of this book comprises the reminiscences of Emily, Lady Clive Bayley, of her life in Moghul Delhi, edited and annotated by M. M. Kaye. The interpolated pages in colour are from the "Delhie Book" of her father, Sir Thomas Metcalfe: it should be noted that his cross references differ from that of the present edition.

First published in Great Britain 1980 by
Webb & Bower (Publishers) Limited,
33 Southernhay East, Exeter, Devon, EX1 1NS

Distributed by WHS Distributors
(a division of W. H. Smith and Son Limited)
St John's House, East Street, Leicester LE1 6NE

Designed by Malcolm Couch

© John Ricketts and M. M. Kaye 1980

British Library Cataloguing in Publication Data

Bayley, Emily, *Lady*
    The golden calm.
    1. Delhi – Social life and customs
    2. British in Delhi
    I. Title   II. Kaye, Mary Margaret
    954'.56'00421   DS486.D3
    ISBN 0–906671–19–1

Phototypeset in Great Britain by Filmtype Services, Limited, Scarborough, Yorkshire

Printed and bound in Italy by Arnoldo Mondadori Editore

Introduction

Lt.-Col. John Mildmay Ricketts MC

When my great-great-grandfather, Sir Thomas Metcalfe, compiled his beautiful collection under the title of "Reminiscences of Imperial Delhie" he was referring, in his use of the word "imperial", to the empire of the Moghuls, whose influence by then had almost vanished. In bequeathing it to his daughters he cannot have visualized his creation, a sort of *tableau vivant* of bygone Delhi, being appreciated by many outside the circle of his descendants.

I was not aware that the "Delhie Book" existed until one day, years ago, when I called for the first time on my widowed great-aunt Constance Clive Bayley. My wife had warned me not to smoke without first asking the old lady's permission. I received a charming welcome and was at once given a drink; and "Wouldn't you like to smoke?" she asked.

"Yes," I replied, "I would love a cigarette, if you don't object."

"Object?" she exclaimed: "I smoke cigars." And she offered me one.

We got on very well, and I felt that she approved of her great-nephew.

Shortly afterwards there arrived at our home a brown paper parcel containing the "Delhie Book" and a charming note from my great-aunt. It read in part: "Knowing India so well, I thought perhaps you would like the Delhi Book, which the Bayley family 'set great store by'. I am sure Clive [my great-uncle, her late husband] would have been only too pleased for you to have it."

I thought the "Delhie Book" deserved a better fate than being securely hidden away in a drawer, seeing the light of day only when displayed on special occasions. The obvious solution was to have it published, using modern methods of reproduction to do justice to the original paintings. And such publication provided the perfect opportunity to bring to light, as an ideal complement, the journal in which my great-grandmother, Emily, had recorded in her own words the story of her time in Delhi. It is a perfect accompaniment to the souvenir her father gave her. Sir Thomas and his daughter are the joint authors of this lovely book, the production of which is their memorial.

These reminiscences should intrigue the scholar and those interested in the character and conduct of our predecessors whose lives were interwoven with oriental peoples and their history. There was an interval of comparative quiet in the era of the British presence in India that was itself but a minute fraction of that country's turbulent record of foreign invasion and internal strife. It was the calm before the hurricane that was to shape the destiny of India for years to come. This book gives us the opportunity to realize some of the fascination of the history of India in what an old Rajput once called "old-king-time".

In 1813 Sir Thomas Metcalfe followed his father Sir Thomas Metcalfe MP into the Indian Service and sailed for Delhi. He spent nearly all his working life in the Delhi Territories, and was Delhi Resident at the time of his death.

The position of the British Resident and Agent to the Governor-General at the Moghul Court in Delhi was an unusual one. It is described by Sir John Kaye in his *Life and Correspondence of Lord Metcalfe*:

> The duties of the Delhi Resident were onerous and complex. The Residents at other Courts were simply diplomatists. They were bound to confine themselves to the political duties of their situation, and to refrain from all interference with the internal administration of the country in which they resided. But the Delhi Resident was at once a diplomatist and an administrator. It was his duty not only to superintend the affairs of the pensioned Moghul and his family, but to manage the political relations of the British Government with a wide expanse of country studded with principalities, ignorant alike of their duties and interests, and often in their ignorance vexatious in the extreme. It was his duty, too, to superintend the internal government of all the Delhi territory – to preside over the machinery of revenue collection and the administration of justice, and to promote by all possible means the development of the resources of the country and the industry and happiness of the people.

This description, of course, applies to the duties of Sir Thomas' elder brother Charles, but things were very much the same during Thomas' time. Indeed, the two brothers seem to have been very similar both in their temperaments and in the performance of their duties, for Emily's account of her father is startlingly like this description by Kaye of Charles:

> The new Delhi Resident was just the man to carry himself bravely as the representative of the British nation at an Eastern Court. His liberality was of the best kind. It was Charles Metcalfe's nature to give freely; he was bountiful without ostentation, and no man ever left his house without carrying with him a grateful recollection of the kindliness and geniality of his host.

To these two brothers, Charles and Thomas, Delhi owed much.

Emily Annie Theophila was Sir Thomas' eldest daughter by his second wife, Felicity Annie, a sister of Sir Sam Browne VC, who raised Sam Browne's Cavalry and invented the famous Sam Browne belt. Felicity died in 1842, aged only thirty-four, leaving two sons and three daughters.

Emily was born in India, but spent her childhood in England. At the age of seventeen, in 1848, she rejoined her father in Delhi, and two years later she married Sir Edward Clive Bayley, then Under-Secretary to the Foreign Department, in St James' Church.

Sir Thomas was to live in Metcalfe House until his mysterious death, from some subtle poison, in 1853. His son Theophilus succeeded to the baronetcy and, at the outbreak of the Mutiny in 1857, was Chief Magistrate in Delhi. Although it is outside the scope of our present purpose, it is of interest to note that he made a miraculous escape at this time from the city, in due course, thanks to a good sword arm and a disguise supplied by his Indian friends, reaching Hansi to report for duty.

But back to Sir Thomas. The putting-together of his reminiscences would have been possible only during a sustained period of peace and quiet throughout the territories which he administered as Resident; and his position as Agent to the Governor-General at the Court of the King of Delhi, together with a detailed knowledge of the people of the city and its surroundings gained over many years, rendered him the ideal person to set about such a work. To him it was a labour of love, to be pursued unhurriedly during spells of leisure; and he set himself the task not just owing to love of his family, to whom he wished to leave a souvenir, but because he himself loved Delhi greatly. It is our tremendous good fortune that he completed his self-imposed task in time for his daughter Emily to rejoin him in their home and provide the family touches and the additional "human interest" which she supplies *via* her Journal.

We can be thankful, too, that he was spared the ghastly happenings of the Mutiny. One can but wonder if he, with his finger ever on the pulse of things, had sensed the beginnings of what prompted Lord Canning to prophesy, at a dinner given by the Honourable East India Company on his appointment as Governor-General in 1855, in the following terms:

> We must not forget that in the sky of India, serene, as it is, a small cloud may arise, at first no bigger than a man's hand, but which, growing bigger and bigger, may at last threaten us with ruin.

In the light of the events of 1857, prophetic words indeed.

The glory of Akbar, the true founder of the Moghul Empire, who reigned from 1556 to 1605, did not rest solely upon his conquests: he was illustrious primarily because of his imperial policy. He sought to weld all the different races of India – Moghuls, Afghans and Hindus – into a united empire. He sought to deal even-handed justice to all classes of his subjects, without regard to religion or nationality.

Akbar was a contemporary of England's Queen Elizabeth. He was strong, active, fond of field-sports and a friend of Hindu princes, whose histories he studied; he was interested in religion, and ordered Persian translations to be made of the Maha Bharata and Ramayana, the great Hindu epics. Neither his son Jehangir nor his grandson Shahjehan inherited his genius; both, however, continued to pursue his policies.

But then there came Aurungzeb, who reigned for nearly fifty years, 1658–1707, from the death of Oliver Cromwell to the opening years of the reign of Queen Anne. And with him began the decline of the Empire. He reversed the policies of Akbar: zealous and bigoted, he restored the authority of the Mohammedan religion and taxed and persecuted the Hindus; as one might expect, this practice resulted in the Rajput and Mahratta princes defecting to form independent empires. Aurungzeb's successors were puppets in the hands of their viziers and, in 1739, the Moghul Empire received a death-blow from the invasion of the Persians under Nadir Shah; henceforth the Empire's influence extended barely beyond Delhi and its surrounding country.

"Delhi is far" is an old saying, and the hard truth of it was to be brought home always to the procession of invaders, including Nadir Shah, aspiring to the conquest of all India. It was an obvious and tempting objective – whether the aim was conquest or mere plunder. Adjacent to Indraprastha, one of India's most ancient sites, Delhi is associated with nearly every era in India's history – Rajput, Mohammedan and Mahratta. Its streets and bazaars have grown up in historic times; their history is told in written annals. But they stand in the midst of relics belonging to the remotest antiquity . . . the remains of a metropolis which may date as far back as the oldest cities known from the ancient world.

The kings, the nobles and the teeming populations have passed away; as Kipling said, cities and thrones and powers are like flowers, that daily die. But as the tide of each dynasty ebbed away so it left behind in monuments of stone – and, more recently, sometimes in paint and manuscript – a record of its art and culture and, as always, of its history. Inevitably, the ravages of time and the Indian climate have taken their toll of palaces, forts, mosques and temples; shamefully, also, neglect has played its part.

Fortunately, where they are preserved, the works of scribes and painters have succeeded in outlasting those of architects and masons – an irony, since hard stone appears far more durable than weak paper. The buildings depicted in Sir Thomas Metcalfe's "Delhie Book", in paintings by the finest artists of his day, are shown as they were before the siege of Delhi during the Indian Mutiny, when the general action caused serious damage to some. Many suffered from inevitable neglect and even, in some cases, vandalism in the years immediately following the Mutiny – in this respect, both British and Indians were not blameless.

In 1872 the Commissioner in Agra, who was responsible for its beautiful buildings, through which he liked to wander in his leisure time, discovered strange goings-on. He had to issue a general order – a difficult one to enforce – forbidding the desecration of the Taj Mahal by non-Mohammedans wearing shoes, and by its use as a favourite picnic spot. On one occasion he surprised someone measuring slabs of marble in preparation for their systematic removal by boat! Later, at the instigation of the Viceroy, the Government carried out a greatly needed programme of restoration and repair to halt the damage to the country's heritage, work perpetuated in subsequent years.

In 1857, India was wakened by the nightmare of the Mutiny – so-called since it initially erupted in units of the Bengal Army. In fact, it was a rebellion on a much wider footing against a regime that foolishly threatened the religions, customs, property and vested interests of vital sections of the civil populations of the north of India. It is a lesson of history that periods of comparative peace loosen the sinews of control when those in higher places, out of touch with the feelings and opinions of the rest of us, are oblivious of signs and mutterings at ground level. The causes of the Mutiny do not concern us here, but we can note in passing that after the outbreak there were faults on both sides.

That said, let us look at a most extraordinary event that took place in

1877. This was the Imperial Assemblage at Delhi at which Queen Victoria was proclaimed Empress of India. The British Empire was the only empire that had ever kept the peace in India and protected her from foreign invasion. The Assemblage was a festival of peace. It was held not at the close of a victorious war but in the midst of a period of tranquillity which, but for the explosion of 1857, had been maintained in India for sixty years. In his speech at the State Banquet Lord Lytton, the Viceroy, said:

> There is one thing above all that the British Empire means. It means that all its subjects shall live in peace with each other. That every one of them shall be free to grow rich in his own way, provided his own way is not a criminal way; that every one of them shall be free to hold and follow his own religious belief without assailing the religious beliefs of other people, and to live unmolested by his neighbour. To preserve the peace we need laws which we must be able to enforce. We must have judges to administer them and police to carry out the orders of the judges; and then we must have troops to protect the judges, the people and all concerned.

We cannot help but applaud the sentiments expressed in this speech.

To most of us art, especially architecture in durable stone, is a vital and absorbing way to learn history. In this book the illustrations of the many buildings, mainly Moghul, and the descriptions of their background to the affairs of those who built them go hand in hand; and seldom can there be found a composition of such beauty of illustration and such excellence of calligraphy. All of these buildings, some of them masterpieces, cannot fail to fascinate the beholder – either as seen directly in their concrete form or as illustrated in this book. Whether a fortified palace designed jointly for pleasure and protection or a mosque for private or public devotion, or a residence, all were conceived in less than a human lifespan with typically aesthetic Moghul endeavour.

Some, in their day, adjoined or even contained their own garden paradises of flowers and cool fountains. A thousand years hence, these relics of a great dynasty may have vanished owing to the effects of natural causes. Their likeness will not be seen again, and their beauties will be recaptured only through pictorial records such as Sir Thomas Metcalfe's "Delhie Book". (In this context it is appropriate to quote a great eastern sage who was once asked by a victorious Sultan to give him an inscription for a ring that was to convey in a few words the advice best calculated to moderate the triumph of prosperous fortune and diminish the misery of adversity. The sage wrote the line: "And this, too, shall pass away." He might well have been describing the relics of the Moghul Empire.)

What have all these deliberations to do with this book?

I have delved a little into the past – into history before the time of Sir Thomas and Emily – to show how government devoid of firmness and tolerance decays for want of esteem and respect. The British came to India originally as traders, not invaders. Their trading rights, freely and honourably negotiated, needed protection from local interference, often instigated by the French in the "cold war" of the time or from competitive Dutch and Portuguese interests. Success in these endeavours to maintain a foothold led inevitably to consolidation and territorial expansion. The influence of the Honourable East India Company spread willy-nilly in direct opposition to the stated policy of its directors in London, who saw their enterprise being gradually made more complicated by factors unconcerned with simple commerce. The Moghul court in Delhi provided no cohesive government over the vast subcontinent, whose peace was riven by intriguing and warring principalities.

As the scale of the Company's involvement increased so its small actions became battles and its battles campaigns. Clive, who had been a clerk, became a general. Parliament appointed Warren Hastings as first Governor-General of Bengal; and, between the victory of Clive at Plassey in 1757 and the quelling of the Mutiny, the process of settling the peace of India went steadily on. From winning a trading post in Surat in 1606 the British had, perhaps without realizing it, acquired an empire, the seeds of which had been germinating for decades before.

Men like Sir Thomas Metcalfe and Colonel James Skinner – "Skinner of Skinner's Horse" – through firm rule and fearlessness in battle had won the confidence and respect of all classes. In the aftermath of the Mutiny swift and summary justice was done, seen to be done, and understood by all: treachery met its just deserts and loyalty was promptly rewarded.

As we have seen, it was with masterly timing, once the dust had settled, that the Imperial Assemblage was staged – a mighty Durbar, understood by all who took part, where, with fitting pageantry and careful ceremony, the princes of India came freely and without fear to offer their loyalty. In time, they and their countrymen twice joined cause with Britain to defend freedom, giving just as freely of their lives and treasure; no man in Britain's Indian forces was ever conscripted.

After victory in the Second World War the process, planned many years before, of the handing-over by the British of the whole of India was accelerated and, on Partition in 1947, the treasures of Delhi became the responsibility of the new government. The restoration to India of the soil on which the Moghuls had built so wonderfully brought with it in terms of real estate an investment priceless to India and the world; with this, for full measure, Britain bequeathed to the new Indian Government as lasting evidence of a benign sovereignty Sir Edward Lutyens' magnificent Viceroy's House.

The spotlight of history has forever shone on Delhi. The Moghuls died of self-inflicted wounds. Britain did not fade away; she handed over an edifice the foundations of which were laid in Sir Thomas Metcalfe's time and, in doing so, left behind nothing of which to be ashamed.

The illustrations in this book were executed by native Company artists working to Sir Thomas' commission. It is of course impossible to identify most of the artists today: the number of Company artists working in Delhi at the time was legion, and many of the pictures are unsigned. Those that are signed in this book are the work of one Mazhar Ali Khan, and there are stylistic reasons for thinking that he painted several of the others. A survey of the Delhi artists carried out some decades later at the instigation of Queen Victoria mentions an Mazhar Ali Khan: whether this is the same man or a descendant is impossible now to determine.

Houses often have a kind of aura, sensed when inside them. There is an atmosphere attributable to the personality of someone who has built his house on a chosen spot and dwelt in it with his family for a spell of time; it is an atmosphere that can permeate the site, come fortune good or bad.

While helping to plan the resistance to the invasion of India by the Japanese I was allotted quarters in, of all places, Metcalfe House. This was my first acquaintance with the place that had been my ancestor's home. Sacked in the Mutiny, it had become an important ruin to be occupied because it was upon a vital point.

In later years a handsome building with spacious rooms and wide cool verandahs replaced it on the same site. The pattern of all had changed, except for two great underground rooms which were filled with lumber; I hear that now they are filled with snakes to deter entrants.

The house seemed to have accepted its fate as though that were no fault of its owner.

There were no ghosts, and it was pervaded by a sort of calm.

For my very Dear Girls
From their affectionate Father

Lehlee
25th Nov 1844
The last I shall
See of my Dear
Child Charles

ALBUM

Reminiscences of
Imperial Dehlie.

Saint James' Church Dehlie

Erected by the late Colonel James Skinner C.B. at his own sole expense, and at a cost of 95.000 Rupees was consecrated on the 21st November 1836 by the Right Reverend Daniel Wilson D.D. Bishop of Calcutta — The text selected for the occasion was well taken from Rev: III. 7. 8.

On the 4th December 1841, the munificent Founder and truly good man was suddenly removed from his sphere of usefulness on Earth. lamented by all, and of the poorer classes by the thousands who had shared his Bounty — His mortal remains were at first consigned to the Cantonment Burial Ground at Hansie, from whence, after a period of 40 days, they were conveyed to Dehlie, escorted by 200 men of his own Regiment of Irregular Horse and were finally deposited in their most fitting resting place, within the Sacred Edifice he had dedicated to his God.

The Funeral Service was read by the Reverend H. Loveday — The 50th Chap: of Genesis was very appropriately chosen for the 1st Lesson, and from the 3. 7. 8. 9 Verses was the Text also taken — "And 40 Days were fulfilled for "him, for so are fulfilled the days of those which are embalmed — and "Joseph went up to bury his father, and with him went up all the Servants "of Pharaoh, the elders of his house & all the elders of the land. & all the house of Joseph "& his brethren & his father's house. only their little ones & their flocks & their herds they "left in the land of Goshen. and there went up with him both Chariots and horsemen "and it was a very great Company."

A suitable mural Tablet has also been erected. at the East end of the Church and on the left of the Altar by the family of the deceased —

This Sacred Edifice
Raised by the pious Munificence of
Colonel James Skinner C.B.
Now contains, at the universal request of his friends
and the Community of Dehlie, his mortal remains,
this Church being Considered by all of them
As the most appropriate resting place for the deceased:
So long as Charity, Benevolence,
And the kindlier feelings of the human heart,
Are held in respect by Mankind
The name of James Skinner will be remembered and revered.
Highly honored and deeply lamented
He departed this life at Hansee
On the 4th December 1841,
And was interred here on the 19th January 1842.
Aged 64.

The *Jameh Musjeed* or the Great Cathedral was erected by the Emperor *Sha Jehan*, commenced in the fourth and completed in the 10th year of his reign, at an Expense of 10 Lacks of Rupees— It is situated about ¼ mile from the Palace— It's foundation was laid on a rocky Eminence, scarped out for the purpose, called the *Jugula Puhar*—

The ascent to it is by a flight of red stone steps 35 in number through a handsome Gateway of the same material— There are three Entrances of the same description to the East, North and South— The Terrace on which the Mosque stands is a square of about 1400 Yards, and in the Centre is a fountain lined with Marble for the necessary ablutions previous to prayer.

An arched Colonnade surrounds the whole of the terrace with Octagon Pavilions at the four Corners— The Mosque is of an oblong form 260 feet in length, surmounted by three magnificent Domes, intersected with black stripes and flanked by two Minarets rising to the height of 130 feet— Each Minaret is ascended by a winding Stair-case of 130 Steps, and has three projecting Galleries of white marble, crowned with light Octagon Pavilions of the same—

No Endowment, as is usual with Mohummudan Public places of Worship, was ever assigned to this Mosque, it being considered the special charge of the Crown— and from the inability of the King to defray the Expense of the repairs, the British Government in 183 expended the sum of Rs in renewing the North Minaret partly destroyed by Lightning.

The Emperor Shah Juhan (the King of the World) was the son of Juhangeer (the Conqueror of the World) and succeeding on the death of his father, took formal possession of the Throne on 28th January A.D. 1628. When firmly established in his Government, he gave loose to his passion for Magnificent Buildings and Expensive Entertainments. He erected Palaces in his principal Cities, and on the first Anniversary of his accession he had a suite of Tents prepared in Cashmere, which if we may believe his Historian, it took two Months to pitch - and on that occasion he introduced new forms of lavish Expenditure, for, besides the usual ceremony of being weighed against precious substances, he had Vessels filled with Jewels waved over his Head or poured over his person (according to the Superstition, that such Offerings would avert Misfortunes), and all the wealth so devoted was immediately scattered among the bystanders or given away in presents. The whole Expense of this Festival, including gifts of Money, Jewels, rich Drapes, Arms, Elephants and Horses Amounted to 1,600,000 £ Sterling. Notwithstanding Shah Juhan's love of Ease and pleasure

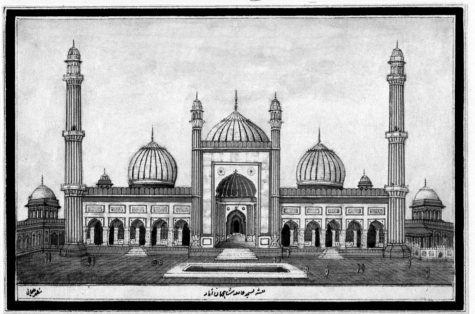

the time spent away from his Capital, and the Erection of those celebrated Structures in which he took so much delight, he never remitted his Vigilance over his internal Government, and by this and the judicious Choice of his Ministers, his Reign was perhaps the most prosperous ever known in India, though often times engaged in foreign Wars, his own Dominions enjoyed almost uninterrupted tranquillity together with a larger share of good Government than often falls to the lot of Asiatic Nations: but nevertheless this able Prince was dethroned by his 3rd son Aurungzeb in A.D. 1658, and unaccountably as it may seem without any of his old Servants attempting to stir in his favor. He was still treated with the highest respect; but altho' he lived for seven Years longer, his Reign ends at this Period.

Shah Juhan was the most Magnificent Prince that ever appeared in India. His Retinue, His State Establishments, His Largesses, and all the Pomp of his Court were beyond all they had ever attained to under his predecessors, and yet they neither occasioned any increase to Exactions nor any Embarrassment in his finances; the most striking instance of his pomp was the construction of the Peacock Throne, so designated from a Peacock with its Tail spread (represented in its natural Colours of Sapphires, Emeralds, Rubies and other appropriate Jewels) which formed the chief Ornament of a Map of Diamonds and

and precious stones, the whole valued at Six Millions and a half Sterling. This splendid Throne was carried to Persia by Nadir Shah on his invasion in 1738/39. Vide page 52.

ﺳﭙﯿﺎﻧﺎ ﻣﺎﻧﻧﺪ ﮔﺎﻧﻪ ﻣﺮﺟﺎ ﺗﻣﺎﻧﺎ

A view from the Rockey Heights above the Military Cantonment. looking toward the City of Dehlie — The artist in his Endeavours to do much. has been more minute than Clear in his delineation. My House. is on the left (No.1) — The Assembly Rooms, a thatched Building in Front. with the City and Principal Mosques in the distance. —

The Tomb of the Emperor Hoomaeoon distant about 5 Miles S.S.E. from Dehly
was erected by his Son the great Akbar, who reigned between the Year A.D. 1556
and 1605.: It is a Square Building of Red Stone – the four Corners inlaid with
white Marble and the whole surmounted by a Magnificent Dome of the
latter material.

It is believed from its Shape to have formed the Model of the more
beautiful Mausoleum of Agra the Taj Mahul, erected by the Emperor
Shah Jehan entirely of Marble, decorated with Mosaics over his
favorite Queen Moomtaz Muhul. the Pride of the Muhul or interior
Apartments. Taj Muhul is a Corruption of the Queen's Name.
the Tomb occupies a Site of 165 feet Square, and the Terrace on which it stands, of
303 feet Square.

Charlie – Teesie
Emmie and I
Spent our Xmas
Day – 1841. here
with the Romains

The Emperor Hoomaeoon succeeded to the throne on the death of his
Father. the Emperor Baber in A.D. 1530. but his Reign was one of continued
Misfortune – In 1537 He was compelled to march towards Bengal to put
down an insurrection raised by one Shere Khan of Afghan extraction:
but whose father held a Jageer in Behar – In 1540 Hoomaeoon was defeated by Shere Shah in a general Action. compelled to fly to Lahore
and subsequently in 1543 took refuge in Persia – In 1545, aided by a force
from Persia, the exiled monarch was enabled to retrace his Steps and
march against Kandahar. which was then held by his Brother Mirza
Askeri, whom he compelled to Surrender. It was not until 1555,
however

however that Hoomaeoon Regained possession of his Capital, and in Six
months after his return, he fell over a Parapet wall and was so injured
that he died on the 4th Day, in the 49 year of his age and 26th of his Reign in-
:cluding the 16 Years of his Banishment from his Capital.

The Golden Calm

The quarter of a century that preceded the Sepoy Mutiny of 1857 saw a gradual easing of the anarchy and violence that had become almost an accepted way of life to a majority of the denizens of India. The power of "John Company" – the Honourable East India Company whose charter to trade with the East Indies had been granted by Queen Elizabeth I – was growing rapidly; and with it their British-officered sepoy army, since trade is not best served by constant affrays. "Suttee", the burning of widows, had been declared illegal, the bands of ritual murderers known as "Thugs" who preyed upon travellers had been hunted down and dispersed, slavery had been outlawed, a Medical College established in Calcutta, flogging abolished in the native (although not in the British) army, and one of the many provisions in the latest Reform Bill stated that "no native of the said territories, nor any natural-born subject of His Majesty resident therein, shall, by reason only of his religion, place of birth, descent, colour, or any of them, be disabled from holding any place, office, or employment under the Company".

There were still famines, risings and mutinies; and no less than three wars: the futile and disastrous First Afghan War and the First and Second Sikh Wars, the last of which resulted in the annexation of the Punjab by the East India Company's Government. But the ancient Moghul capital of Delhi, together with its immediate surroundings, had enjoyed a halcyon period of calm that to its inhabitants, both Indian and British (not least among them the Great Moghul himself, Bahadur Shah, last Emperor of Delhi, and his friend the Resident, Sir Thomas Theophilus Metcalfe, who represented the British Power at his court), must indeed have seemed golden.

The British Resident of Delhi received a large monthly allowance from the Company's Government, not only to enable him to keep what amounted to a court of his own, but – as my kinsman Sir John Kaye wrote of the previous Resident, Sir Thomas' brother Charles – "to support it in becoming splendour". This Sir Thomas most certainly did. Having arrived in India as a young man and spent most of his life in or near the Moghul capital, he regarded Delhi as his home and acquired land there: an estate consisting of over a thousand acres that had previously been farmed by Gujars, a tribe who are gipsy-folk by origin and who were not best pleased at being evicted when their village, together with its croplands and grazing grounds, was requisitioned and either sold or given to the feringhi (foreigner). It was here, near the banks of the Jumna River, that Thomas built Metcalfe House – a magnificent, porticoed palace which he crammed with treasures, surrounded by trees, artificial lakes and beautifully laid-out gardens, and where in due course his wife, Felicity Annie, bore four of her six children. Only two of them, Emily, her eldest daughter, and Charles, her second son, were not born in Delhi; Charles being born in Simla where his mother had probably gone to escape the hot weather, and Emily – Emily Annie Theophila Metcalfe – in Meerut, a garrison town less than fifty miles from Delhi.

There is still a Metcalfe House in Old Delhi: a long, white mansion with a high, many-pillared verandah. But although it stands on the same site it is not the one that Thomas built, for when the Mutiny broke out in May 1857 the Gujars took a belated revenge and destroyed it, together with its contents. But by that time Thomas had been dead for three and a half years.

As a child, I myself knew the second Metcalfe House well, because my father had his office there in the time of the First World War. There were also a number of children's parties held in its grounds, and I can remember, too, being taken there by my mother, and told to sit in a corner and try not to be tiresome while she and a great many other British and Indian women rolled bandages or cut lint for the wounded, and packed it into endless boxes that were sent to the Red Cross or to various Military Hospitals.

Not far from the walls of Delhi, on the nearest corner of what was once the Metcalfe Estate, stood Maiden's Hotel; a building that must date from well after Metcalfe's day. But near it, on the opposite side of the long road that leads to the Kashmir Gate, is Ludlow Castle, built in Sir Thomas' time and, judging from the picture that he had painted of it for his "Delhie Book" (see page 174), still looking very much as it must have done when he was alive. In my day, this was the Delhi Club – later the "Old Delhi

Club". Now it is a college. But in a corner of what was once the Club lawn (and which, when I last saw it, was the playing fields) there still stands one of the engraved stone plinths that marked the sites of the siege batteries used in the final assault on Delhi in September 1857.

My childhood memories of Delhi are not so very different from those of the child Emily, for I too remember the kind, faithful servants, and the river where, of an evening, our Ayah would take my sister and myself to play on the silver-white sands and paddle in the shallows. The birds that Emily remembers would have been the direct ancestors of those that were so familiar to us: doves, parakeets, satht-bai (which means "seven-brothers", but which we had always known as "seven-sisters", because they hop about in groups of seven, twittering together like a group of excited schoolgirls), koils, hoopoes and egrets, the grey-headed crows of the plains, blue-jays and peacocks. Oh, darling Delhi – what a magical place you were for children!

*M*y early recollections are all confined to my home at Delhie, where I spent most of my infancy – the beautiful house – the river – the birds – the kind faithful old servants have never been forgotten, but I do not remember any events beyond the nocturnal visit of a large wild cat who somehow got into my mother's bedroom and drank up a cup of tea by her bedside. This must have been when I was between three and four.

The next event was my Uncle Clem Browne's marriage to Miss Davidson, which took place in my father's house when I was four years old, and I also remember an accident to my sister Georgie, who when about two years old was roughly pushed off the sofa in the drawing-room by a little playfellow and broke her collar bone. The bone was set by Dr Mark Richardson, for whom both my sister and I always entertained much affection all through his life. He was a great and valued friend of both Father and Mother and had been associated almost from the beginning with our old Indian home.

Then, in February 1835, my sister Eliza was born, and I can well remember the curiosity with which we inspected her, and enquired where she had come from?

Soon after this occurred the event which I clearly remember to this hour, and though I was then only four and a half it made such a deep and lasting impression on me – the murder of the Honourable

William Fraser, Commissioner and Resident at the Court of the King of Delhie.

It was Sunday evening, March 22nd 1835. Georgie and I were sitting in the Bay Drawing-room with Mother, who was instructing and reading to us – how clearly I remember her that evening, sitting between us! My Father was sitting in the Napoleon Gallery, a room dedicated to the memory of the Great Napoleon, of whom he was a great admirer. It was full of books and pictures of Napoleon at all periods of his history, and contained many valuable bronzes, busts and relics of him (although many of these were collected in later years). The whole house was still and hushed as only an Indian house can be, when suddenly there were sounds of great stir amongst the servants, and my Father came hurriedly into the room where we were sitting and announced Mr Fraser's death, and that he was going out at once to enquire into the murder.

How well I remember clinging to my Mother, and her horror at the news – and our childlike fears for our Father's safety, because if Mr Fraser had been murdered, perhaps Papa would be killed too! We heard the carriage drive rapidly away and we sat by our Mother who was silent, and remained there until Father's return. I shall remember that day I think as long as I live. In that same room where we were sitting hung a coloured print of Sir Joshua Reynolds' well-known picture of two children's heads, one fair and one dark, and I suppose this event fixed that picture and its position indelibly on my memory, for I never forgot it.

I can distinctly remember, too, old Colonel Skinner, and the Begum, his wife, who gave me my Indian dress – they were both in Delhie at this time – and I also remember that later on in that same year we had to leave our home at Delhie, Georgie and I, to travel with our dear Mother to Calcutta, preparatory to going to England.

This would have been Colonel James Skinner, the famous "Sekunder Sahib", who married an Indian lady, built the church at Delhi and raised and commanded Skinner's Horse, a cavalry regiment nicknamed the "Yellow Boys" – not because they were yellow in the modern meaning of that word, but because of the colour of their uniforms.

Skinner's mother had been Indian, and his exploits not only would fill a book but have in fact filled several; the latest of which, *Skinner of Skinner's Horse*, by Philip Mason – that Arthur Bryant of the Raj – will well repay anyone who is interested in learning more about this fabulous character. His regiment is still going strong, and it is to be hoped that many Skinners will grow up to command the "Yellow Boys" in the years to come.

In 1947, when India became independent, James Skinner's sword, on which each new recruit took an oath of allegiance to the regiment, was brought back to England by the British officers who had served in Skinner's Horse, and presented to the National Army Museum to put on display. But it has recently been returned to the regiment "on permanent loan", so that now, once again, newly joined troopers of that famous regiment will be able to touch "Sekunder Sahib's" own sword as they are sworn in.

I cannot remember any details of that time, except the last evening spent in the old house and the parting from my Father – his kissing me as he put me into the palanquin (covered doolie) at the foot of a flight of stone steps leading down from the verandah. I remember Georgie being carried down in the arms of an old servant and myself going down holding my Father's hand, and my dear Mother crying when my Father kissed her and said "Goodbye" to us. The crowd of old servants cried too and made many Salaams, and the old Ayahs kissed our feet.

That scene is quite fresh in my memory, and when I returned as a girl of seventeen to that beloved home I pointed out the staircase and place of farewell to my dear Father, who acknowledged the correctness of my memory.

I have a hazy recollection of some of the incidents of our long journey to Calcutta. It was made partly by land in palanquins and partly in boats – "budgerows" as they were called – covered barges built of wood, painted green and very comfortably furnished and divided into two rooms each – for sleeping and sitting rooms. A separate "budgerow" was fitted up for kitchen and servants' use – and this small flotilla kept company together and proceeded quietly and peacefully down the stream of the great rivers, sometimes towed by men walking on the river bank, sometimes rowed by boatmen on board, sometimes sailing with the wind – but always stopping at sundown, moored to the bank of the river with men posted as "chokidars" or watchmen to take care of the little flotilla during the night.

When I and my sister were taken home, we left Delhi by train instead of travelling by road or river as Emily did. But although the "budgerows" she speaks of are no more, I too have been lucky enough to spend two weeks drifting down the Ganges by day and making camp at nightfall, and I feel sure that the great river and the enormous land must have looked almost exactly the same to her as it did to me – except that in her day there would have been many more boats to be seen, because until the advent of steam and petrol the rivers served as highways. Perhaps when petrol runs out they will do so again.

I remember some of the quiet days thus spent, and the howling of the jackals at night on the river bank; the occasional stoppage at a large station or town on the river and the visits of the snake-charmers, conjurers and toy-sellers, which delighted us much. I think the journey from Delhi to Calcutta in those days down the stream took about two months.

My next recollections are of a large bedroom in Government House, Calcutta, where we stayed with my uncle Sir Charles Metcalfe (later Lord Metcalfe), then acting Governor-General of India. Our dear old servants Moonia Ayah, and Khajoo Khansamah, and Mohammed Buksh the khitmutgar were with us there. I remember the green sward round Government House and the large round stone balls at the side of the carriage drive up to the house – these I recognized years after, in the same place.

I have memories of my loved Mother reading and praying with us, and of her sweet face in a general way; although not of distinct features. But I have thought of her so much and so earnestly all the years of my life, that I have fashioned in my own mind a very vivid picture of her.

My uncle too I remember well – and his presenting Georgie and me with two beautiful workboxes made of rosewood. They were lined with red silk and fitted with silver articles, and being much too good for children's use were kept very carefully treasured for many years – only looked at on high days and holidays, until we were old enough to use them carefully. How we treasured those boxes for years! They were the receptacles of all our special treasures as children, and I grieved sorely over the loss of mine in the Mutiny at Delhie, where it was sent for safety during our absence from India.

Oh! how Georgie and I treasured some Indian coins – gold mohurs and rupees – one of each, given to each of us in Calcutta. We looked at them on particular days during our childhood with reverence and love as part of our Indian belongings. 🪳

We too, my sister Bets and myself, took back to England with us a box full of treasures to remind us of the land that we looked upon as "home" and were being sent away from. But our treasures were not in the least like Emily's and Georgie's. There were no gold mohurs or silver rupees among them, and the box in which we kept them was not of rosewood lined with red silk, but a cardboard one that had once held three cakes of Erasmic Soap. The treasures we kept in this consisted of bits of gravel, a neem leaf, flakes of sandstone, river-sand, pebbles, dried flowers, a few pieces of bark and a parrot's feather – each item carefully selected from some specially loved spot to be kept as a memento and treasured for years.

*I*n Government House in those days I remember all my uncle's ADCs (aides de camp), Captain Higginson (now Sir James Higginson) and John Smythe.

I do not remember the parting from my dear Mother except in a vague hazy way. But it must have been some time in February 1836 that she put us – Georgie and me – on board the sailing ship "Broxbourneherry" for England. We were consigned to the care of a dear old servant, Phoebe Saunders, whose fortunes had been associated for years with my Mother's family. She took devoted care of us and has always been a true and faithful friend. The Captain of the ship, Captain Chapman, had us under his special charge, as also had Mr Robert Saunders, an old friend of my Father's.

We had a cabin on the port side of the upper deck and I remember to this day the disposition of the berths and furniture in it. Mr Saunders had the large State Cabin on the lower deck, and every day I used to go to him for a reading lesson according to his promise to Mother. I learnt the first part of the Fifth Chapter of St Matthew while on the voyage, from the Bible given to me by Mother.

A few of the incidents of the voyage round the Cape of Good Hope remain in my memory: the capture of a dolphin and its glittering colours as it lay on deck, the noise and fun amongst the 🪳

sailors on "crossing the Line" – an old custom now I believe fallen into abeyance; the anchorage at St Helena, and the road on which we drove up the Castle hill when we landed for a few hours. I have never seen a picture of St Helena that I can remember, but I still have a vivid recollection of the place as seen from the ship.

Our voyage came to an end some time in June 1836, when we landed at Weymouth. Many years elapsed before we saw Captain Chapman and Mr Saunders again, but Georgie and I always liked to talk of them and to remember all their kindness to us. And when we did see them again, many years afterwards, they took great interest in us and were always kind to us both for our dear Mother's sake.

Phoebe Saunders had fulfilled her duty to us to the very utmost, and after landing at Weymouth, she conveyed us by coach to Clifton to our Grandmother, Mrs Browne, who was to have care of us.

This dear old lady was then living in Saville Row, Clifton, with her old friend Mrs Lawrence – mother of my Uncle George Lawrence. Into that house we were both lovingly welcomed, and I can remember nothing but love and kindness and sweet affection from my Grandmother during all the years we were under her care. She was a sweet, tender-hearted, gentle old lady who never wearied of caring for her "little children" for their Mother's sake. Both souls and bodies were carefully tended and instructed, and I remember so plainly even now a little black-bound Prayer Book from which I used to read the evening prayer, "Lighten our Darkness", as I knelt on a chair by the open window in Grandmama's bedroom before I went to bed, she sitting by me and helping me to read.

We were ultimately to be consigned to the care of my aunt, Mrs Smythe, my Father's sister – who already had charge of our brother Theo. But as it was not convenient for her to have us at once, we continued for some time with Grandmama. We were very anxious to see Theo and at last were taken to Mrs Bragge's School at Clifton for a meeting with him, although as he was only just recovering from some infectious illness – measles I think – we were not allowed to kiss nor shake hands, but could only look at each other from a distance. I recollect him quite well as he stood on the doorstep and we on the gravel path in the garden: a stout, chubby lad wearing a large white turned-down collar with a frill round it, white drawers of the same model with deep frills round his ankles, a little dark

Continued on page 49

The Emperor Buhadoor Shah.
1844

A Nanuck Punthee or follower of
the Seick Devotee Nanuck, a
Religious Mendicant.

فقير

The Roshun oo dowluh Musjeed is situated within the ward of the Chandnee Chowk or Principal Street, and contiguous to the Kotwal's Chabootra – It was here that Nadir Shah in 1738/9 gave orders for and witnessed the massacre of the inhabitants of Dehlé – Tradition says that on Saturday the 10th of the Moon, and the Anniversary of the Eed ool Zoha,[1] and about noon some Horsemen were detached to Puhar Gunj[2] in the Environs of the City to open the Granaries and fix the price of Corn – Wheat was sold at 10 Seers[3] the Rupee,[4] but this not being to the satisfaction of the proprietors, they assembled a Mob in which the above Horsemen and several Kuzzulbash[5] were killed – The tumult increased, many of Nadir's Troops were cut up on the Ret or sand between the Palace and river – On Sunday 11th March about 8 in the morning when the tumult was at its height, Nadir came from the Palace, proceeded towards the Chandnee Chowk, and went into the Roshun oodowluh[6] Mosque, when there one of his Officers was killed by his side by a shot fired from some of the houses in the neighbourhood and designed for Nadir – a general slaughter was ordered which lasted till 3 OClock in the Evening, and extended in one direction from the Oordoo Bazaar[7] in front of the Palace to the old Eed Gah,[8] 3 Coss[9] distant – in another to the Chitee Qubr[10] and in a third as far as the Tobacco Mundavee[11] and Pool Metaiee Ke-[12] About 400 Kuzzulbash[5] were killed and 120 to 150,000 of the Citizens slaughtered – The Massacre was stayed by the orders of Nadir, at the intercession of the King Mohumud Shah, and the Minister Nizam ool moolk-[13]

1	One of the Chief Mahomedan Festivals	7	A Market
2	Name of a Place, literally: the Hill Market Place	8	A Building appropriated to Religious Sacrifices.
3	A Corn measure - a Seer is equal to 2 lb.	9	1 Coss is equal to 1½ Miles. Eng: measure.
4	The current Coin nominally 2/6 of our Money	10	A Street so named. Qubr means a tomb.
5	A description of Persian Soldiers, Literally Red Cap.	11	Tobacco Mart
6	Light of the State. A nobleman in the Reign of the Emperor Mohumud Shah.	12	Bridge where Sweetmeats are sold
		13	Regulator of the State

The unfortunate Emperor Mohummud Shah in whose Reign this dread:
:ful Tragedy occurred, succeeded to the Throne in A.D. 1719, on the deposition
and Murder of his Cousin the Emperor Furrooksier. Each successive day
brought some fresh proof of the decline of the Royal House of Tymoor -
while the indolence and dissipation of the Emperor disgusted his Mi:
:nister both able and willing to conduct a vigorous administration.
Mutual aversion ensued and the latter resigned his office and return:
:ed to his own Possession in the South of India, where he established
himself as an independent Chief.

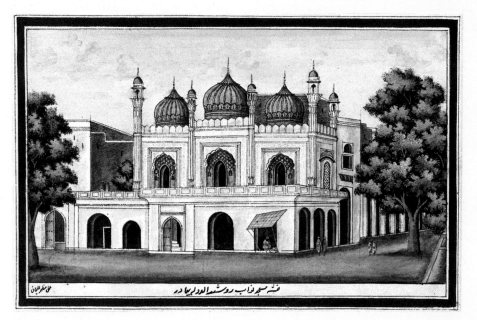

فتہ مسجد نواب روشند الدولہ بہادر

In 1737, Dehly was attacked by a Mahratta Army under Bajee Rao
the Pirshwa, literally a Leader, and a Sally by the besieged was driven back
with heavy loss. Reinforcements however arriving, the Mahratta was induced
to retreat, and the former Minister Asoph Jah having returned, was invested
by the Emperor with full Powers. Nadir Shah having usurped the Sovereign:
:ty of Persia, advanced upon Candahar as well as Ghuznee and Cabul, and
which he conquered
in November of that Year, advanced within 100 Miles of Dehly. The Emperor
Mohummud Shah at last rousing himself from his supineness exerted himself
to collect a force, and having been joined by his Minister Asoph Jah, hurried
to Kurnaul and occupied a fortified Camp.

Sadul

Sadut Khan (the propitious chief) the Viceroy of Oudh arrived in the neighborhood of the Camp in support of the Emperor; about the same time with Nadir Shah. A general Engagement ensued. Asoph Jah the Minister from real or pretended Misconception stood Aloof. The imperial Army was routed. The Commander in chief Killed. Sadut Khan taken prisoner and Mohummed Shah compelled to offer his submission, and repair with a few followers to the Persian Camp.

In 1739. March, Nadir and the Emperor entered Dehly, and both took up their abode in the Palace. The Massacre has been already described, but the sufferings of the People did not cease with this tragedy.

Nadir Shah's sole object in invading India was to enrich himself by its Plunder. He took possession of the Imperial Treasury and Jewels including the celebrated Peacock Throne. Seized on the whole Effects of some great Nobles, and compelled the rest to sacrifice the larger part of their property as a ransom for the Remainder.

The inferior officers and Common inhabitants were then constrained to disclose the amount of their fortunes and pay accordingly. Great numbers died of the usage they received and many destroyed themselves to avoid disgrace and torture. At length having exhausted all the sources from which Wealth was to be obtained, he reseated Mohummed Shah on the Throne, invested him with his own hand and quitted Dehly. after a Residence of 58 Days, carrying with him Treasure in Money to 9 millions Sterling Several Millions in Gold and Silver Plate and Jewels to an amount inestimable. For some time after Nadir's departure, the inhabitants of Dehly remained in a sort of Stupor; Many of the Houses were in ruins. Much of the City was entirely deserted and the whole infected by the stench of the bodies which lay unburied in the Streets.

The Minister Asoph Jah died in 1748 at the age of 104 Lunar Years and in the same year, the Emperor expired within a month after hearing of the battle of Surhind gained by his Son Ahmed, over the Dooranee chief of the same name.

منظر کوتوالی چبوترہ دہلی

The Kotewals Chubootra, alluded to in the second line of the preceding Page is situated in the Principal Street, and adjoins the Roshun ood Dowlah Mosque before described.

The Building is appropriated to the same purpose now, as previous to the introduction of the British Rule. The Kotewal being the Chief native Magistrate of the City. He has sub-ordinate to him 52 Police Officers, 148 foot Soldiers and about 230 Guards at the several Gates, who are also available for Police Purposes. All these are paid by the Government. For the Protection of the City at Night, we have a watch of 400 Men paid by the people. The principal Gates are ten in Number, with four smaller Out-lets or Wickets. The Streets are 377 in Number. Of these Eleven are Main Streets of good Width. They contain 246 Mosques. 147 Hindoo Temples. 23,462 Dwelling Houses of which 17,564 are of good substantial Masonry. The Shops are estimated at 9720, but only 7,662 are occupied by Dealers. There are 91 Hindoo and 29 Persian Schools. 31 Burial Grounds. 2 Public Serais or Halting places for Travellers. 667 Wells, of which 52 only yield good Water and 10 extensive gardens.

The Population is estimated at 120 or 30,000 Inhabitants, of which the Mohummedans and Hindoos are nearly equal, if any thing, the latter preponderate.

The subjoined is a view from the Terrace of Mr. Metcalfe's House of a Portion of the Palace of Dehly built by the Emperor Shah Juhan and of the Pattan Fortress of Suleim-Gurh, constructed by the Emperor Suleim Shah, Son of the Pattan adventurer Shere Shah by whom the Moghul Emperor Hemaioon was temporarily expelled from the Throne of Dehly. The latter must have been built about the Year A.D. 1539.

The Bridge connecting the two, although in some degree assimilating to the Patan Style of Architecture was built by the Emperor Shah Juhan at the same time with the Palace.

The Name Suleim-Gurh being associated with Recollections derogatory to the dignity of the Imperial House of Temour, is never mentioned in the Royal presence or used in Correspondence to and from His Majesty. That of "Noor Gurh" or the Fortress of Light being substituted.

N.B. In this I am incorrect. I have lately seen the Inscription on the Bridge to the purport that it was built by the Emperor Juhangeer (conqueror of the world) the Father of the Emperor Shah Juhan about the Year A.D: 1607.

مشتر یہ نمبر دہلم گرد قلعہ شاہجہان آباد

The Emperor Buhadur Shah.

The Prince Aboo Zufr or the Victorious was the eldest Son of the late Emperor Mohummed Ukbur Shah the 2nd. born in the Year A.D: 1773, and succeeded to the fallen dignity of the once mighty House of Temour on the 29th of September 1837. The father having demised at the Kootoob late in the Evening, it was necessary to await the arrival from thence of the several Emblems of Royalty before the Installation of the Successor could take place. It was therefore Midnight when the Ceremony was performed by the Agent to the Governor General in the Tusbeah Khana or Oratory adjoining the great Hall of Audience. The Prince on his accession assumed the Style and Title of Buhadur Shah. He is Mild and talented but lamentably Weak and Vacillating and impressed with very Erroneous Notions of his own importance, productive of great Mortification to himself and occasionally of much trouble to the Local Authorities –

قلعه جنتر منتر جیدن دروازه اجمیری

The Observatory at Dehly denominated the "Juntur-Muntur", literally Witchcraft, was Constructed by the MahaRaja Jey Singh of Jeypoor who succeeded to the inheritance of his Father about 1693 of the Christian Era.

It is situated without the Walls of the City at a distance of 1½ Mile SW, and consists of several detached Buildings.

The principal ones as shewn in the annexed drawing are the Gnomon, a large Equatorial Diab, and a Circular Building designed for the purpose of observing the Altitude and Azimuth of the heavenly Bodies.

The two former do not require particular Notice, but on the third of which there are two similar and exactly close to each other, and intended not as duplicates but as supplementary to each other. a Pillar rises in the Centre of the same height with the Building itself, which is open at the top.

From this Pillar at the Height of about three feet from the bottom proceed Radii of Stone horizontally to the Circular Wall of the Building.

These Radii are thirty in Number. the Spaces between them are equal to the Radii themselves, so that each Radius and each intermediate Space forms a Sector of Six Degrees.

The parts in the Center Pillar opposite to the Radii and in the intermediate Spaces, in all Sixty, are marked by lines reaching to the top, and were painted of different Colours. As no Observation could be made in the one Building when the Shadow fell on the Space between the Stone Radii or Sector, it was found requisite to construct the Second on which the Radii or Sectors correspond with the Vacant Spaces of the other. So that in one or other, an observation of any body Visible above the Horizon, might at any time be made.

At Benares and Oojein. Similar Observatories, though not on so large a Scale were constructed by the same Scientific Individual.

Camels unloading after a days Journey.

An Indian Stable

دربار محمدلان بادشاه خاصیت موربت لاعلوی دابر عمران پان مصر دارهل

His Majesty the late Emperor Akbur Shah holding
his Durbar or full dress Court on the Jushun. the
anniversary of his accession to the Throne —

The Suwarree or Royal Procession of His late Majesty Mohummd Akbur Shah, the 2d. — who succeeded his Father the Emperor Shah Alum in November 1806, and died at the Kootub in September 1837. Aged 81 years.

A mild and Benevolent Prince, but more fitted to reign under the Protection of the British Government, than in the troublesome times of his unfortunate Father and his immediate Predecessors.

Akbur Shah left issue 11 Sons and 6 daughters, and was succeeded by his eldest son the present King Ba= :hadar Shah

The leading Elephant of the Procession with the Chuttah or Umbrella, the Chief Ensign of Royalty and which no one else but the Sovereign is permitted to assume. —

سوار فیل گرسنه بادرنبار علیه

The 2nd Elephant of the Procession - Bearing the Royal
Standard - Green being the National Color of
the Mahomedans -

A Shooter Sowar or Camel Rider with the
Nuhara or Kettle Drum - A necessary
part of a State Procession -

A Party of the 1st Irregular Cavalry or Skinner's Horse. well known by the familiar name of Yellow Boys, from the Color of their Uniform – A splendid Corps raised by the late Colonel Skinner C.B. and at one time

Consisted of 3000 men – Change of Rulers, and the Interest of others deprived the Gallant Colonel in later years of the 2/3d of this Body, who were Either disbanded or formed into a separate Regiment under a separate Commandant –

The Dewan-e-Khass or Audience Hall for the Nobility, was constructed by the Emperor Shah Juhan, by whom the Royal Palace was also built. It is situated at the upper end of a spacious Square, Elevated upon a Terrace of white Marble about four feet in height. The Dewan-e-khass in former times was adorned with excessive Magnificence, and though plundered by Nadir Shah, the King of Persia during his invasion in 1738/9, and Subsequently Mutulated by the Barbarous Hordes of Mahrattas during the latter End of the past and beginning of the present Century, still retains sufficient Beauty to render it the object of Admiration.

The dimensions are said to be 150 feet in length by 40 in breadth. The Roof is flat supported by numerous Columns of white Marble, richly ornamented with inlaid flower Work of different Coloured Stones, chiefly Cornelian. The Cornices and Borders being decorated with Frieze and Sculptured Work. The Cieling was formerly incrusted with a rich foliage of Gold and Silver Work throughout its whole Extent. This during the Period of Anarchy was removed and an imitation Ceiling, which still exists, substituted.

In the interior of the Building and in the Cornice are the following Lines written in the Persian Character in letters of Gold.

اگر فردوس بر روی زمین است
همین است و همین است و همین است

Ugur Firdoce bur Roo-e Zumeen ust.
Humeen ust o Humeen ust o Humeen ust.

If there be a Paradese upon Earth.
It is this. it is this. it is this

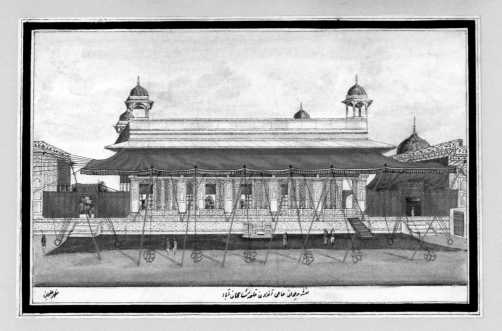

نقشه دیوان عام آنطوری خلعه شاهجان آباد

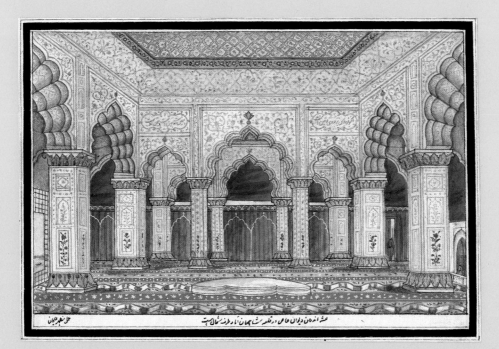

نقشه اندرون دیوان عام ور قلعه شاهجان آباد طرف شمالی است

Zumbooruckchee or Camel Artillery men
from Zumbooruck, a piece of Ordnance of small
Calibre

Dohleh or Covered litter in which a Bride is con-
veyed to the Bridegroom's House

Mode of Conveying Females on a long
Journey or through arid Countries —

نایچ طوالف

Nautch or Dancing Girls.

frock and stout leather shoes. Mrs Bragge's round red face surmounted with a huge cap with frills rose behind him, and with her large hands laid upon his shoulders, she explained to him who we were. 🌿

During the period of British rule in India (which was very brief when one compares it to the length of time that the Roman invaders held power in conquered Britain), hundreds of thousands of British children who were born in that country grew up barely knowing their parents. And year after year weeping mothers took their children down to the great trading ports of Calcutta, Madras and Bombay, and handed them over to the care of friends or nurses to be taken "Home" and brought up by relatives, or in many cases (Rudyard Kipling and his sister Trix among them) by strangers. Such separations were one of the saddest aspects of the Raj; almost sadder than the terrible toll that heat and disease took yearly from the British who lived in India, and the fact that every mother expected to lose at least three children out of every five she bore – Emily herself was to lose a son and a daughter out there. India was littered with the graves of children, and as a result those who survived infancy were sent home and often did not see their parents again until they were almost grown up: if ever, since many parents, like Emily's mother, died before their children were old enough to go out to join them.

There are touching letters dating from 1838 from Emily herself, writing in England to her parents in India, one of which reads: "My own darling Mama: I was very glad to receive your kind letter dated 17th July 1838 I have got an exercise for the Hip and Grandmama says she thinks it is better I have sent you Eli & Charlie a present The Penwiper and kettle for you, the India Rubber Ball for Eli and the soft Ball for Charlie Grandmama gave me tenpence a week & I saved it up & had £.10s.d. to spend I bought them in the Soho Bazaar I like London very much J'apprends L'anglais, le Francais, la Musique et la Danse I send my love to all & to Dr Richardson.

"We are going to have a dinner in our dinner set on Theos birthday Good bye my own darling Mama Your affec^{te} little Girl Emily."

With a similar disregard for punctuation, Emily appended a brief note to her father: "My own darling Papa: I must write to you, as I have not done so for a long time and hope that you will accept of a pair of slippers from both of us I saw Aunt Sam Swinton the other day Adieu mon cher Père Your affec^{te} little Girl Emily."

Nor did such separations happen only in the eighteenth and nineteenth centuries. They continued right up to the Second World War, when it was suddenly discovered that children *could* remain in India and receive an education there without being ruined by the spoiling of Indian servants, or falling victims to cholera, typhoid, smallpox, malaria, heat-stroke or similar ills. Although, of course, by then medicine had learned to control most of these perils, including hydrophobia and snake-bite. My own brother was left in England to be brought up by relatives when he was only six years old, and I remember my mother weeping over the photographs of him that were sent out to her, because the boy in the studio portraits was not the one she had known. I and my sister were luckier, since girls were not sent "home" as early as boys. But my brother was twelve before he saw any of us again. And then he did not recognize us.

My husband, too, was only four when he was left behind with a family of maiden aunts in Ireland, who spoiled and adored him, and whom he somewhat naturally regarded, and always will, as his collective mothers. He had comparatively little use for his own, whom he hardly knew and looked on as an interloper – a stranger. The wives of Indian-service officers and all British officials paid a heavier price for serving the Raj than anyone nowadays realizes.

Emily was not yet six and Georgie only four when their mother kissed them goodbye on the deck of that sailing ship in Calcutta, and since Emily seems to have no recollection of her brother Theo he must have been sent home when she was very small and he very young, and all too soon Eliza and Charles would be sent home to join them. Poor Lady Metcalfe – poor Felicity Annie, née Browne! How you must have grieved to see them go and wept over their stilted little letters. Yet you were only one of thousands who had to endure that same cruel grief.

*P*hoebe Saunders remained with us while we were with Grandmama, but when later on in the same year (1836) we were consigned to Aunt Smythe's guardianship, we parted from her and had a Nursery Governess, Miss Halse, who was very kind to us, and who commenced our education. We lived with our aunt at 41 Royal York Crescent, where we had a large bedroom on the drawing-room floor, overlooking the back garden – a strip of melancholy, unkempt, mouldy ground leading to the coach house and stables from the back dining-room which also served as our schoolroom.

My uncle, Mr Smythe, was a perfect specimen of the old-fashioned clergyman. He was tall and thin, very courteous and kindly, with grey hair on his temples and the sides and back of his head, but a bald patch right on the top. When not otherwise occupied, his right hand and arm were always raised to his head, and his second finger used to describe slow circles on the bald patch! This habit used to cause us all much amusement, for wherever he was, he used to sit or stand with his left hand in his pocket and his right hand raised as I have described – especially was this his custom when in Church listening to the sermon, during which time he sat with his head bowed on his chest and closed eyes.

I remember him so well, and I loved him much; he was so kindly, and I never heard a cross word pass his lips. He lived much by himself in the front parlour which was his sitting-room; he break-fasted there alone with my aunt, had his luncheon by himself, and dined there with my aunt only. We children – my cousin Emily, Georgie and I – took all our meals in the back room with Miss Halse; my aunt only joining us at our dinner hour of one o'clock.

It was a much stricter régime than we had been accustomed to with our grandmother, as Aunt Smythe was a great disciplinarian. Not that we objected to that, but she was by nature stern and rather suspicious, and made the great mistake of not believing children's words. She was so afraid that they would be untrue that she was always on the look-out for a falsehood, and constantly caused us to prevaricate because we knew our word was not trusted. This was the principal mistake in her system of government, although in other ways we were very happy, for she was so very clever and accomplished that she could always teach us something new – or sing or play to us, for she was a perfect musician. She also had a great knack of amusing children, and to this day I look back with a keen sense of pleasure to the evening hours spent with her when she used to teach us to sing "Little Boy Blue" and other songs.

At that time my dear Aunt Mary – then Miss Browne – was at school at the Miss Rogers' in the Crescent; and a sweet-looking girl she was – always so kind and loving to us. We used to meet occasionally, and I was always told that I was *someday* to go to the same school. But meanwhile we did our lessons with Miss Halse, who was an efficient teacher for young children. We used to enjoy our walks on the Clifton Downs, and many many happy hours did we spend roaming about there, and looking down on the Avon, and climbing the zig-zag path up the cliff.

My cousin Charles Smythe used to be at home occasionally, and those were happy days for us: he was so good and clever and affectionate that he was loved by us both – and got us out of many scrapes, for he was idolized by his mother and his word was law to her. He was a youth of rare promise, both morally and intellectually, and if he had lived would doubtless have been a man of mark. But he died at the early age of seventeen in 1841, and never was one so young more deeply mourned by all who knew him.

We spent several months with our aunt, Mrs Smythe, and from the first day of our residence with her our musical talent was cultivated by her daily performances to us on the piano and harp, in both of which she excelled. We were always in great glee when summoned to the drawing-room to hear her play the harp, for it was a room otherwise used only occasionally, when there were visitors or, rarer still, for entertainments. The furniture was generally wrapped in swaddling clothes of brown holland, but there was a carpet worked in squares of two feet, each of a different pattern, by my aunt and a number of her friends, and this carpet was a never-failing source of pleasure and interest to us while we listened to my aunt's performances.

During this period of our lives we were much thrown in with some of the members of the Lawrence family. There was old Mrs Lawrence, mother of Sir George and Lord Lawrence, a fine-looking, tall old lady of whom we stood in considerable awe, although she was always kind to us. But she was a disciplinarian and looked like a "Roman" mother of warrior Sons! Her unmarried daughter was Charlotte, whom we have always liked, and with whom we have been involved at different periods of our lives. ❧

For some unknown reason, Emily neglects to mention that the "'Roman' mother of warrior Sons", who had no less than eleven sons, numbered among them Sir Henry Lawrence, the "Lawrence of Lucknow" who was one of the best loved men in India. It was Henry who not only had the idea of starting a school-cum-orphanage for the children of British troops serving in India, but managed to raise the money to get it built and endowed. The Lawrence School at Sanawar, near Kasauli in the Simla hills, still flourishes in Independent India, and has made a great name for itself. It is to Henry, too, that the Frontier regiment known as the Corps of Guides owes its existence, since the Corps was another of his ideas. His tact, kindness and skill as an administrator succeeded in pacifying the defeated Sikhs, and he made himself so loved that when he left the Punjab he was accompanied for many miles by a host of chiefs, Sikhs and Punjabis who had become his friends, and followed by a great crowd of ordinary people of all ages who wept because he was leaving them. Given time, he might even have pacified the great province of Oudh. But he was sent there too late, and died in its capital city of Lucknow in the second month of the Mutiny – killed in the besieged Residency. Henry has always seemed to me the best of the "India Lawrences", and I find it surprising that Emily never once mentions him.

*A*nother daughter, Mrs Bernard, wife of a Dr Bernard, a physician at Bristol, was a hard, rough-mannered, coarse woman, with a kindly heart. We used to see her and her children sometimes – they were a remarkably plain family, but in later years her son Charles distinguished himself in India as a good officer and is much liked by those who know him well.

Dr Bernard was consulted by my Aunt about a naevus, a growth on my neck under my left ear, which I had had from my infancy, but which had lately developed into larger proportions and caused me much pain and inconvenience. Dr Bernard recommended pressure being applied systematically, to reduce its size, but as he did not seem certain of curing it even after this treatment, my Aunt did not consent to placing me in his hands.

Sometime during the spring of 1837, my cousin Emily and I were sent as daily scholars to the Miss Rogers' School where my Aunt Mary was still a pupil, but I did not appreciate this at all. The formal schoolroom, the dry bread for lunch, the stiff schoolmistresses and the awe with which they were all regarded were distasteful to me, although I liked some of the girls we knew there; the two Miss Caldwells – Catherine and Ellen (the former became Mrs Hamilton and is mother of the present Lady Dufferin).

There were also the two daughters of the Count and Countess of Montijo; Pakita, afterwards Duchess D'Alba, and Eugénie, who afterwards became Empress of the French. The elder was very dark and handsome, a complete Spaniard, but Eugénie was of a Scotch type – fair, freckled and with bright red carrotty hair which hung down her back in thick plaits. She gave no promise of the marvellous beauty of her after years, but it has always been a puzzle to me how such very red hair lost its colour and became the sandy colour that afterwards became her so well. We saw a great deal of these girls then, for their mother, previously Miss Kirkpatrick, had been an old friend of my aunt's and it was at her recommendation that they were sent as day boarders to Miss Rogers' School at Clifton – the Count and Countess residing meanwhile in one of the houses in the "Paragon".

The two girls used often to come and spend the afternoons with us and have their dinner with us out of our children's toy dinner service, and much amusement was caused by Eugénie on one occasion eating up the whole leg of mutton.

The Count we held in great awe, for he had only one eye, the other being disfigured either by nature or accident and giving an evil look to his face. But the Countess was a jolly, good-natured woman, and little did she or anyone else in those days dream of all the triumphs and vicissitudes that were to mark her daughter Eugénie's life.

I remember that it was in June of this year that one day, when I was at school and talking to Eugénie, William the Fourth's death was announced. And afterwards came all the grand doings at the Proclamation of the Queen's Accession – the triumphal processions, etc., etc. 🪰

Reading Emily's remarks about Eugénie, one is tempted to retort: "*Miaow*! Oh Emily, you little cat!" For it is clear that Emily – a beauty herself and not ashamed of saying so, as you will see from a comment by her later on, when she describes herself as being one of several "very handsome" bridesmaids! – did not think much of the younger daughter of the "evil" looking, one-eyed Count de Montijo and his "jolly" Scottish wife.

Her verbal sketch of Eugénie is far from complimentary, while the surprise she expresses as to how the "bright red carrotty hair" could ever have turned the colour it did (even then she will not call it "blonde", but prefers to describe it as "sandy-coloured"!) suggests that she suspects Eugénie of tampering with nature. In which she may have been right, for "bleaching" did not come in with peroxide, but has been practised for centuries; Italian beauties in the heyday of the Borgias found that mule's urine did the job very nicely. Yet Eugénie de Montijo, despite freckles, carrotty hair and greediness (that leg of mutton!), was considered one of the most beautiful women of her age, and one has only to look at contemporary portraits of her to see why this was so; even after making allowance for the flattery of royal portrait-painters.

But although she married Napoleon III, became Empress of France and presided for many years over the most brilliant court in Europe, her life was far from happy. When the French were defeated by the Prussians at the Battle of Sedan and the Second Empire collapsed in ruins, she and her elderly husband (Louis Napoleon was eighteen years her senior) took refuge in England, where the ex-Emperor died in 1873. But life had still not done with the widowed Eugénie, for six years later a final blow was dealt her when her only child, the young and handsome Prince Imperial, who had begged to be allowed to see some of the fighting in Africa during the British campaign against the Zulus, was killed in Zululand.

It is disconcerting to realize that Eugénie herself, a close friend of Victoria, lived on until the nineteen-twenties – into the "Jazz age" – dying two years after the signing of the Armistice that ended the First World War.

*T*he summer holidays of 1837 were spent with our dear "Grannie Browne" at Tenby, in South Wales.

I have never been back to Tenby since, but I remember the place so well and have always had a great desire to revisit it. The Castle Hill and the walks on it, the wonderful sands and rocks and bays, the expeditions we made to Guelden Island and other places, are all fresh in my memory still. "We" included, of course, my sister Georgie and my brother Theo. Our Governess, Miss Halse, had accompanied us to Tenby in order to relieve our Grandmama of taking entire charge of us, and it was she who used to take us for walks and bathing and on all our expeditions.

I shall remember one day there as long as I live. We were all out with her on the long, beautiful stretch of beach on the west coast, digging with our spades and making sand castles on a summer afternoon while Miss Halse sat and read. The tide was out, and oblivious of the fact that it would of course come in again, we played on; until all of a sudden we found that we were almost surrounded by water.

On three sides at least we were cut off from returning, and only by climbing the precipitous rocks could we reach a place of safety! I well remember our Governess' horror at our situation, and our fright. But Theo took in our danger at once, and without counting the cost rushed through the advancing tide, keeping close to the foot of the rocks, and ran into the town to give notice of our position and to get help.

Miss Halse screamed after him to return, fearing he might be drowned, but he gave no heed and disappeared from our view. There was nothing to be done but to climb to a place of safety as fast as we could, and although this looked at first an appalling task I suppose danger gave us courage and strength, for with our Governess' help we climbed and held on, until we got to a grassy slope high up, where we felt we were safe.

How well I recollect my heart beating with fear and excitement; and then our rapid walk home, as the evening was drawing in and we did not know our way across the fields. When at last we arrived at the door of our lodging, our servant, Meade, cried out with surprise and joy at seeing us, and told us that Theo had rushed up to say that we were all drowned and my poor Grandmother had run out in frantic despair to get assistance. Meade immediately ran out after her and succeeded in bringing her home quietly, and Theo too, and that evening, as you may well imagine, was one of great excitement.

After the summer holidays we again returned to Aunt Smythe's care at Clifton, and while we were in her charge Theo always spent his holidays with us. He was a bright, active boy, but he was not happy either at the schools chosen for him or with the Smythes. They were too strict for a high-spirited boy who needed loving home influence and affection.

Sometime during the autumn I went with my Grandmother on a long journey by coach, through Bath and Devizes to London, as it was deemed necessary to consult both Dr Guthrie and Sir Benjamin Brodie about the naevus on my neck which was rapidly increasing in size. I remember the visits to both the two surgeons; Guthrie recommended continuous pressure being applied to disperse it, but Brodie said it must be taken out by operations, which rather startled my Grannie, as he did not hide from her that they would be very severe. She asked him if Guthrie's plan could not be tried first, and he said: "Of course it *can* be tried – but the swelling will grow more and choke the child, and then of course I can do nothing."

We left London without any decision being arrived at, but soon after my return to Clifton it was decided to place me under Sir Benjamin Brodie's care, and so in November or December I again went to Town with my grandmother, and our first fortnight was spent in my great-aunt Mrs Trotter's house, Connaught Place West, Hyde Park. She was my grandmother's sister, and was deeply attached to my Mother, who had lived with her much during her youth.

My great aunt was at this time a widow and very rich. She lived with her only unmarried daughter, Jean Trotter, and was very *grande dame*, and I admired her stateliness greatly. She was also a clever woman of the world – quite the opposite of my dear Grandmother who was sweet, gentle and unsophisticated – but she was extremely kind to me, and I shall *always* remember her with grateful recollection. I fully enjoyed the luxuries and charms of her delightful house facing the Park.

I recollect as if it were yesterday Sir Benjamin Brodie's first visit to perform the operation of putting a "seaton" through the naevus. It was done in the large dining-room in an arm-chair, with my back to the windows, and I fixed my eyes on a full-length portrait – an oil painting by Grant of Sir Henry Lindesay Bethune, my aunt's son-in-law, which hung on one side of the room. The pain was intense while the threads were being passed through, although nothing to the pain of the later operations.

Sir Benjamin praised me for my pluck and Grannie soothed me with her love and sympathy. But I was *very* low, and ten days of suffering continued until Brodie came again and extracted the threads. Then there was a reprieve for a time; during which we removed into lodgings, 41 Beaumont Street, Portland Place, where I spent many weeks of keen suffering – as well as some hours of happiness, cheered by dear Grandmother and Aunt Mary. I shall never forget Brodie's kindness and goodness to me, or that of Meade. And it was this time of constant intercourse with Aunt Mary that cemented an intense affection which lasted all through her life, and made her a second mother to me.

Meade was our personal servant, a good, faithful, kind woman who helped to care for me during the weeks in which I lay on a little bed between my Grandmother's bed and the fireplace.

The winter of 1837–38 was a bitterly cold one and long remembered as one of intense suffering to the poor, and I can still recollect the cries in the streets as the voices rose up to our windows of "frozen-out" gardeners and other miserable sufferers. And I remember too seeing dear Aunt Mary dress for her first ball, with Meade and Grannie putting the finishing touches to her dress at the glass in my bedroom. She was going out under Eliza Melville's chaperonage, and looked very sweet and fresh. ❧

Mary's ball-gown, at that date, would have been in the mode that was replacing the skimpy, flimsy fashions of the Directoire and Regency period. Since muslins and gauzes had gone out, it would probably have been made of heavy silk with an overlay of chiffon, and lavishly trimmed with lace, embroidery or artificial pearls. The bodice would have been tight, high-waisted and low-necked, with puffed sleeves. Ribbons or a sash would have been tied just below the bosom, above a much fuller skirt that widened towards the hem and stopped just short of the ankles, showing a few inches of stocking and satin slippers tied on with criss-crossed ribbons. Victoria had only recently become Queen, and the crinoline, which is so associated with her reign, did not appear upon the scene until over a decade later, when it was made fashionable by the Empress of the French, Emily's one-time schoolmate Eugénie de Montijo, who is rumoured to have had it designed for her in order to disguise the fact that she was pregnant; although this, like many rumours, may be untrue.

I had some severe operations performed in the months of December and January. One I particularly remember – of long steel needles full of caustic being run into the naevus and turned round in it, by Brodie. The agony was too intense for me to speak or cry, and I fainted afterwards. How I stood it I know not! In those days chloroform and ether were unknown, and I have often wondered since how a child's strength had power to endure such suffering. It makes me shudder even now, when I recall it!

There were several operations before the blood vessels were all destroyed and disconnected with the system, and I remember Brodie's satisfaction when one day he handed to my Grannie a small lump, and told her he had succeeded in destroying it. But the ❧

position of the naevus – just below my left ear – was a very critical one, for its close proximity to the carotid artery rendered its removal very difficult, and it had increased so rapidly in size that Brodie had some doubt as to the success of the operation. But it was beautifully done, and when years after he saw me, and inspected the spot, he expressed great satisfaction and said it was as nice a bit of work as he had ever done!

It is sometimes difficult to realize that as recently as our great-grandparents' day – or even, for many of us (myself among them), our grandparents' day – operations had to be endured without the aid of any anaesthetics, and that even very young children had to suffer the agonies that Emily underwent during the removal of that large and disfiguring mole on her neck. It is still a wonder to me that they survived the shock, and it reinforces my view that people as a whole were a good deal tougher in those days. Emily was only seven years old at the time, yet you will notice that she did not scream or struggle, but set her teeth and endured it.

*D*uring some of the many weeks (four months I think) that I was under his care, I suffered also from rheumatic gout and was rolled up in medicated wool. He used to try and cheer me in my sufferings by stories of old gentlemen with gouty toes, and he had always a kind smile for me.

My great-aunt, Mrs Trotter, used to send delicacies to tempt my appetite, and my Aunt Smythe used to write me long cheery letters telling me of my darling Georgie, who had been left with her at Clifton. She also sent me a little book of poetry at this time which I have treasured all my life, and I learnt, while I lay on my bed, "We are Seven", "Casa Bianca", the "Battle of Blenheim" and many other loved poems.

When Brodie pronounced me cured and I got strong enough for the journey, I returned to Clifton, and the Spring of that year, 1838, was ever memorable for the return of our uncle, then Sir Charles Metcalfe, from India.

He was Aunt Smythe's idol, so of course after an absence of nearly forty years his return was a cause of much rejoicing, for he had gained a great public reputation in addition to his many estimable qualities which endeared him to his family. We children remembered him well, having seen him only two years before in Calcutta; and indeed he never seemed to me to alter to the day of his death.

He had a most kindly face, as far as features were concerned although he was a very plain man and moreover had several large warts dotted over his face and forehead. A "Metcalfe" blemish. [*This may account for the growth on Emily's neck. It was probably hereditary.* MMK]

He came by sailing vessel round the Cape and, landing I think at Bristol, came direct to my aunt's house, 41 York Crescent, Clifton. We were turned out of our big room for him, but where we lodged meanwhile I don't remember. Soon after he arrived he gave us each handsome gold pencil cases, and I have treasured mine to this day, and shall bequeath it to one of my children as a very valued relic of him.

Sometime during this Spring too, my aunt Lady Ashbrook [*another Emily Theophila: the family name of her husband, Viscount Ashbrook, was Flower, which is why her daughter was Charlotte Flower and not Charlotte Ashbrook* – MMK] and her daughter Charlotte Flower arrived from Italy at Clifton, and the meeting with my Uncle was a very happy one.

Aunt Ashbrook was a remarkably handsome woman, most agreeable and a beautiful harpist, and Charlotte was then in all the radiancy of her youth – twenty years old, tall and of fine figure, with deep blue eyes, black eyebrows and hair, a brilliant colour, laughing white teeth and red lips. She also possessed great charm of manner and was accomplished, witty and clever, and I conceived a deep admiration and affection for her which I shall always retain. She took an especial fancy to me then, and was always a loving and true-hearted friend until her death in 1850.

Soon after my uncle's arrival preparations were made for his removing to Fern Hill, near Windsor, Berkshire, the family estate which he inherited with the baronetcy, and where he and all the family lived in their youth with my grandfather and grandmother. He at once filled his house at Fern Hill to overflowing with relatives and friends. My Aunt and Uncle Smythe and their children Charles and Emily, Lady Ashbrook and Charlotte, the Brownriggs and their daughters, the Higginsons and their children and many others were soon settled there and lived on him, so that his proverbial hospitality, remarkable even in India, was most freely taxed. But as he cared nothing for "show" but only for comfort and the society of his friends, he thoroughly enjoyed this style of life. However, after a time the tax on his finances became too great, for he was not a rich man for a country gentleman, having spent almost all his official income in India. But he had allowed his portion of £10,000, inherited from his Father, to accumulate during all his residence of forty years in India, and this, with some small amount of savings and his pension from the Government, constituted his fortune at that time. 🐾

Back in the last century, people who were comfortably off and owned large houses (presumably staffed by large numbers of servants or, in the Southern States of America, slaves?) apparently thought nothing of putting up hordes of relatives and friends for visits lasting not only a few weeks or months, but sometimes for years. Such lavish hospitality seems to have been a feature of the age. Yet one cannot help feeling sorry for poor Uncle Charles; and even more sorry for the army of servants who must have been worked off their feet looking after these locusts – particularly those ill-paid and put-upon "slaveys" whose task it was to toil up and down endless flights of back-stairs carrying cans of hot water for basins and baths, and then emptying them again. No running hot and cold water in *those* days.

*B*efore he left India, the Civil Service had subscribed and presented him with a magnificent Diamond Star, which cost £5,000, to wear as his jewelled badge of the Grand Cross of the Bath, in testimony of their appreciation of his services as Governor of the North West Provinces and acting Governor-General of India. He was looked on in those days as the most distinguished member of the Civil Service of India, and although he was not a brilliant statesman, nor a good speaker, he still possessed all the qualifications which were required for a first-rate administrator of the Indian Government, and in his subsequent appointments as Governor of Jamaica and Governor-General of Canada he equally displayed the same capacity for government, combining with great love and power of work much shrewdness and ability, great tact, patience 🐾

and control of temper, and considerable knowledge of men and their characters whether European or native.

My sister Georgie and I spent many happy weeks during this Autumn of 1838 at Fern Hill with our new governess, Miss Sanderson. We had a bedroom with an alcove for one bed, and a small addition to the room in a closet for washing apparatus, which delighted us much. I have visited this room in later years, since Fern Hill became the property of Lady Errington, and found it un-changed, as also the rooms occupied by Aunt Smythe and Emily and our little sitting-room downstairs off the Hall.

In these days I thought Fern Hill was a paradise, and I quite understand my Father's great love for this home of his childhood and youth. He had left it to go to India before he was sixteen, and had always cherished the hope of returning there in his old age; although that alas! was never to be, for he died at Delhi at the age of fifty-eight; on November 3rd 1853. But the grand old tree just outside the park gates under which he used to play as a child still survives, and the place is full of memories sacred to him and to his parents, brothers and sisters.

When we left Fern Hill, we went with our governess to live with dear Grannie Browne at 17 Portland Terrace, a row of small houses outside Regent's Park, not far from St John's Church and the Marylebone Cricket Ground. We were very happy here, as we always were with Grannie. Our ménage was a very simple one: our life, our pleasures and our dress equally simple. Such a contrast to the fashions and habits of children fifty years later! Our greatest excitement was a visit to the Zoo, and once we were overjoyed by a sight of Prince Albert when he came to an entertainment at Lord Hertford's house in Regent's Park. This was the Prince's first visit after his engagement to the Queen.

We spent six months in Portland Terrace and changed our governess from Miss Sanderson to Mademoiselle Rivière – we liked both of them. During that time Uncle Sam came to see his mother, Grannie Browne, and played with us, which was a great joy. He also made me eat my first oyster and made me very sick!

This is the Sam Browne whom I mentioned several times in *The Far Pavilions*. He became a Commandant of the Corps of Guides and later of the Punjab Irregular Force, won the Victoria Cross for valour, lost an arm in battle and ended up as Lieutenant General Sir Sam Browne, VC, GCB, KCSI. It was he who invented the Sam Browne belt, so that he could draw his sword with one hand (which was something that had previously not been possible, as the sword-slings of those days necessitated the use of both), and also raised the famous Indian Army regiment that still bears his name – Sam Browne's Cavalry.

We used to take a daily walk with Grannie, and on one occasion I remember her getting a letter when out walking, that told her of the death of her brother Samuel Swinton. We were walking along the path by that long stone wall near the Regent's Park Canal at the time, and I remember that there were posters advertising *The Pickwick Papers* pasted up on it.

On our Mother's birthday, May 14th 1839, we got as presents a Prayer Book and Bible in small purple morocco cases. How proud we were of them. I have one of the books to this day. Then we heard that we were to go to Clifton to stay six months with Aunt Smythe, as Uncle Charles Metcalfe had left to become Governor of Jamaica, and Grannie was to go and live with her daughter Mrs George Lawrence, who was to arrive in England from India in June with her tribe of small children – George, Letty, Bella, Charlotte, then a small baby, and Aleck, about two.

We lived at Clifton for six or seven months, and then went up to Baker Street, London, to spend the Christmas holidays with the Lawrence family and Grannie. But we did not like it at all, for our little cousins were much spoiled, and so in January we moved into lodgings with Grannie at 56 Oxford Terrace, Hyde Park.

Here one day a lady called and interviewed Grannie, and spoke very kindly to us, and when she had gone Grannie told us she was Mrs Umphelby and that in future we were to live with her in Suffolk, as our dear Mother had written from India to say that she had heard so much of her religious training and loving care from friends that she wished us to be brought up by her.

I was then only 9½ and Georgie 7½ years of age, but I can still remember the dress Mrs Umphelby wore when she came on that visit to Oxford Terrace. It was a "chalis" dress, something like cashmere, having a black ground with an orange twirligig pattern on it, and a pelisse trimmed with fur. Georgie and I thought it a very smart frock! We cried bitterly at the thought of leaving dear Grannie, for she was such a darling old lady and we were so happy with her. But when once we got to Belstead and felt Mrs Umphelby's loving influence we never shed another tear.

We arrived at Belstead on January 30th 1840, after a long and tiring journey of sixty-eight miles by coach. The coach came to a stop at the end of a long lane where a carriage was waiting to meet us, and in it we drove to Hill House, Belstead, which lay about a mile off. And as we were desperately tired, we were both soon fast asleep in the two snow-white little beds in Mrs Umphelby's room, in which we were to sleep for some years.

It was not long before we were happy and at home with our playfellows, Emily de Montmorency and Lila Umphelby, who were about our own ages. There were also several bigger girls – Amelia Charlesworth, Maria Beddome, Jane Cowell, Margaret Jennings, Catherine Ashford, and Ellen and Annie Orford, all of whom were very kind and good to us. Mrs Umphelby's parents, Mr and Mrs Shepherd, also lived in the house and managed the farm and household. They were such dear old people, and always so good to us: he a gentleman farmer of the old School, courteous and kindly, and she a very clever and sprightly old dame.

It was a simple old-fashioned farmhouse, with lattice windows – plainly furnished. There was a good lawn and two large horse-chestnut trees with seats under them, where we used to have tea on summer days. The sitting-room windows looked out on a good kitchen garden where there were prolific strawberry beds, luscious pear trees, gooseberries, cherries and currants in abundance. The maid-servants were all country lasses – simple, good, hardworking girls with white caps, red cheeks and bare arms – all in perfect subjection to stringent rules, but supremely happy. Bread-making, butter-making, small table beer brewing – all was done in the house, and "early to bed and early to rise" was the motto for daily use.

Morning and evening prayers were held upstairs for the children, and presided over by Mrs Umphelby, and for the servants by Mr and Mrs Shepherd, downstairs. The food, although simple, was always ample and good, and the greatest excitement was either a tea picnic in Bentley Woods in Summer, or a tea party in the garden on Gala Days – namely birthdays of the children or birthdays of their parents in India – at which times plum and seed cakes and syllabubs of cream were to be had in profusion!

Continued on page 81

The Durgah Qudum Shureef or Shrine of the Holy Foot is situated about One Mile to the N: W: of Dehly. It is so denominated from a Slab within the Building said to bear the impression of the Foot Print of the Mohummudan Prophet Mahomet.

The Tradition is that in the time of the Emperor Feroze Shah - about five Centuries ago - a celebrated Devotee and a Disciple of the Emperor's was deputed to Mecca (to which all True Mohummudans are bound to make one Pilgrimage, if they hope for Salvation) to obtain from the Caliph of that Place a Khillut or Dress of Honor.

The Boon was granted, and in addition as a mark of high consideration the Slab in question was also consigned to the Care of the Devotee.

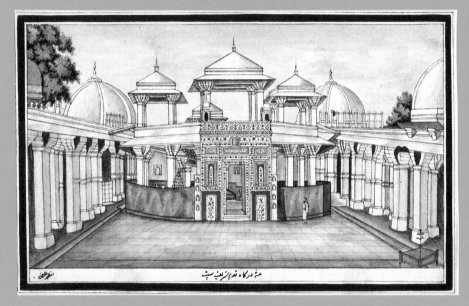

It was brought to Dehly. The Emperor and all his Nobles proceeded to a distance of 15 miles from the City to do Honor to this precious Relic. it was escorted with much Pomp and finally deposited by order of the Emperor in the Royal Treasury. Subsequently the Prince Futteh Khan, a Son of the Emperor having been permitted to Select from the Treasury what he deemed most valuable, claimed possession of the Relic. The Emperor refused to bestow it, considering it as his own exclusive Property: but decreed that it should be placed over the Remains of the one who should first demise.

To the Prince's lot it fell and the Emperor fulfilled his Promise - and around the Grave has arisen this celebrated Shrine - Commenced by

Feroze

Feroze Shah but enlarged and Embellished by successive Kings and Men of
Piety.

Originally it was intended to form the Sepulchre of only men of exalted
Rank or of great Sanctity. In modern times but few of either are to be found
and consequently the exclusiveness had been much entrenched upon. Of those
of later days who have been interred there was the Nawab ShumsoodeenKhan
of Ferozepoor who instigated the murder of the lamented W. Fraser. His body
having been conveyed direct to the Shrine from the scaffold on which he
met an ignomenious Death.

"Mimicks, imatating Nautch or Dancing Girls.

الله اکبر نواب صفدر جنگ بهادر

Mohummud Mokeem (his father being of inferior note) was the Nephew and son-in-law of Nawab Sadut Khan, Boorhan[a] ool Moolk Governor of the Province of Oudh, in the time of the Emperor Mohumed Shah Vide Page 12. On hearing of the prosperity of his father in law in Hindoostan, the subject of this Memoir, came from his native town of Nyshapoor in Persia, and obtained employment in the service of the Emperor, as (Meer atushee) Head of the Ordnance Department with the title of Abool Munsoor Khan, Sufdur[c] Jung, Punj hazaree. Commander of 5,000.

After Boorhan ool Moolki death, having redeemed the promise under which the deceased had pledged himself to pay to Nadir Shah two Crores of Rupees 2 Millions St Sterling. he, Sufdur Jung was installed Viceroy of Oudh in succession to his uncle and father in law.

On Achmud Shah Doorrani's incursion into Hindoostan in AD 5740, Sufdur jung accompanied the Prince Achmud Shah Adest son of the Emperor Mohumed Shah to Surhind, where they met and defeated the Doorrani; The Prince when on his return to Dehly & received Intelligence at Paneeput of the Death of the Emperor his father. Sufdur Jung accordingly prepared the Paraphernalia of Royalty. presented the same to the Prince, and congratulated him on his accession to the Throne of

a. Chief of the State
b. Victorious Manager
c. Warlike

Dehly

Dehly, the Prince thereupon conferred on him the Office of Wuzeer or ✝ Minister.

The Nawab Bahadoor (his real Name being Jawud) one of the favorite attaches of the Court, having aspired to the Office of Prime Minister, was on the Emperor's return to Dehly invited by Sufder Jung to a consultation on State Affairs at the House of the latter, and there treacherously put to death. This occasioned a breach between the Emperor and his Minister, which ended in open Rupture. The Minister attempted, but unsuccessfully to raise an obscure individual to the Throne. While Soorij Mul Jaut, the chief of Bhurtpoor, taking advantage of the Anarchy and Confusion, and instigated it is well known by the Minister attacked Dehly and plundered the City.

In AD. 1751, a reconciliation took place between the Emperor and his Wuzeer. The latter obtained leave to return to Lucknow, where he died. His Remains were brought from thence and interred in the Neighborhood of Dehly, about 5 Miles to the West and Midway between the City and the Kootoob. Shuja ood Dowlah the Son of the deceased raised the beautiful Mausoleum now extant at an Expense of Three Lacks of Rupees.

It is built of the Bofsee Sung. or light Salmon coloured stone. and is surmounted with a marble dome of peculiar Shape and elegance. The Building is 106 feet long, the same broad, and the raised Terrace on which it stands 176 feet in length, by 176 in breadth.

نقشه دروازه مبارک

A Picturesque Gateway near Hoomaion's Tomb. Page 9. and leading to Nizam oodeen Shrine. Page 40.

It is generally admitted that Architects from Europe were employed in constructing the Magnificent Palaces of Agra and Dehly. If any doubt exists, let the annexed facsimile of a Mosaic at the back of the Throne in the Dewan-e-Aum or Public Hall of Audience for the Nobility be accounted for.

It is unquestionably a representation of our Orpheus and from the description of the Instrument, the Cremona as certainly taken from the design by the celebrated Raphael who flourished between A.D. 1483 and 1520.

The animal genus, rudely as they are depicted, complete the Identity. But above all, so little do the Natives of Dehly comprehend the Meaning of the Figure Via, that they have designated it the Miriam or the blessed Mary, the Mother of our Saviour. a proof that, they even believe the work to have been executed by a foreigner, for no heathen could have designed a representation of the Nature they suppose it to be—

N.B. Properly Mareem, the Virgin Mother of whom the Muhammedans speak respectfully, but often Confound with Miriam, the Sister of Moses.

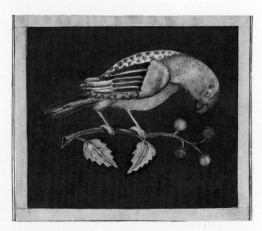

The Tusbeeh Khana or Oratory is situated to the South of
of the Hall of Audience and immediately connected
with the Female Apartments.

It is now commonly used for the mere pri:
:vate Durbars or Levees, but originally, from the Scales
and the Sword Blades, the Emblems of Justice, it was
evidently appropriated to Purposes of higher Import.
These Symbols are by no means of oriental Character and
they consequently confirm the Belief, that the Royal Palaces
at Dehly and Agra were designed and Superintended
by European Architects.

The small Jill Wickit, seen in the 2nd of the
two Drawings and which represents the interior of the
Tusbeeh-Khana, was constructed in the days of Anarchy
and distrust and for the purpose of Communicating to
the Emperor any Secret Intelligence of great Moment, and
at the same time of protecting him from any sudden
Surprize on his own Person.

The Seat in front is the one now in use, but
the Pillows are sadly executed. The long round one supports
the Back and the two smaller ones, the Knees. His Ma:
jesty, be it remembered, is accustomed to sit with his
legs crossed before him. It was in this Building and on this Throne
that His present Majesty was installed at Mid night of the 23rd September 1837
The Guard of Honor on duty on that occasion was commanded by Captn now Major
Thompson C.B. the distinguished Officer of Engineers, who blew open the Gate of the
Fortress of Ghuznee when attacked by the British Army in 1839. and thereby
paved the way for the successful issue of our first Campaign in Afghanistan.

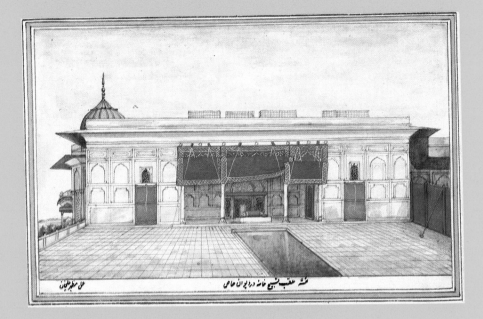

علی مظهر علیخان   نقشه عقب نشیج خانه دربیوان خاص

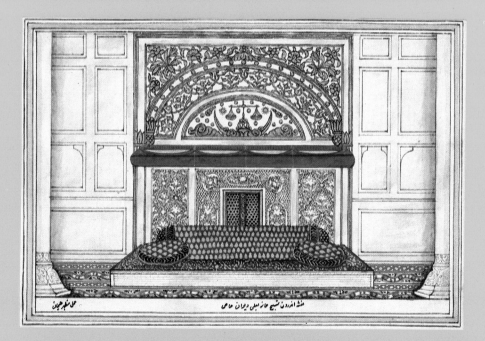

علی مظهر علیخان   نقشه اندرون نشیج خانه نبیل دیوان خاص

William Fraser Agent to the Governor General of India and Commissioner of the Dehly Territory was assassinated within a few Yards of his own Residence on Sunday Evening the 22nd March 1835, about ½ past 7 ô'block when returning from a Visit of Ceremony to Maha Rajah Kulluan Singh Chief of Kishenguah, then residing in our City.

The act was committed by one Kurreem Khan noted as an excellent Marksman and employed by the Newab Shumsood deen Khan of Feroze-poor for this very purpose.

The Assassin rode up in the rear of his Victim and when nearly in a line discharged the contents of his Carbine into the right side. Death instantly ensued. One slug having passed quite through the body, while two others perforated as far as the outer Skin of the opposite side.

Kurreem Khan was executed on the 26th August following and the Newab on the 8th of the following Month, and never was the hand of Providence more signally displayed than in the means vouchsafed to the Local Officers of Government in unravelling this daring deed of Villainy.

The Remains of this estimable and deeply lamented Individual were at first interred in the Burial Ground within the City but subsequently removed to within the Area surrounding St James' Church by the old and faithful Friend of the deceased Colonel James Skinner C.B. by whom also was Erected this Suitable Monument.

The Remains
Interred beneath this Monument
Were once animated
By as brave and Sincere
A Soul
. As was ever Vouchsafed to Man
By His
Creator.
A Brother in Friendship
Has caused it to be erected
That when his own frame is dust

سنگ قبر ولیم فریزر صاحب بهادر

It may Remain
As a
Memorial
For those who can participate in lamenting
The sudden and Melancholy loss
Of One
Dear to him as Life
William Fraser.
Died 22ᵈ March 1835.

As Agent to the Governor General, William Fraser, in the year 1814 accompanied the Army under the Command of the late Major General Sir Robert Rollo Gillespie K:C:B. destined to act against the Hill Fortress of Kalunga.

Though employed merely in a Civil Capacity he volunteered and was most forward on both the unsuccessful attacks on the Fort, and in both instances was severely wounded. In the first of these, the Major General fell. On the second Colonel Mawby of H: M: 53.d Commanded, and although a Breach had been made he was unable to carry the place by assault. it was subsequently evacuated.

The most noble the Marquis of Hastings K:G: Governor General and Commander in chief in India soon afterwards conferred on William Fraser the Local Rank of Major in the First Regiment of Irregular Horse, Commanded by his truly sincere and Excellent Friend Colonel James Skinner, C:B: and in Virtue of this commission, he was present with his Regiment at the Memorable Siege of Bhurtpoor in 1826. and indeed struck the first blow, having been detached in advance of the Army to prevent the Enemy from filling the Ditch of the Fort from an adjoining Lake. He successfully carried out his orders but was slightly wounded in the Skirmish.

Years of Peace having resulted from the glorious success of our Arms at Bhurtpoor. Fraser had no further opportunity of Evincing that daring I may say that utter Fearlessness of Character, which render this device & Epitaph, taken from the East end of his Tomb, most truly Appropriate

The following are two Views of the Palace at Dehly from the River or east
side. The first includes the whole length of line from the Shah Booj, or
Royal Tower on the Right to the Ufsud Booj on the left. Ufsud literally
signifies a Lion: But as tradition does not in any way connect this Animal
with the Building in Question, the latter may be properly denominated the
Tower of Strength.

In the Second are shewn a portion of the Dewan e Khafs or Hall of Audience
on the Right. The Summun Booj or Octagon Tower in the Centre, a very favorite
apartment of the present King – and in which all interviews with the Agent of
a strictly Private nature are held. On the left, the female apartments

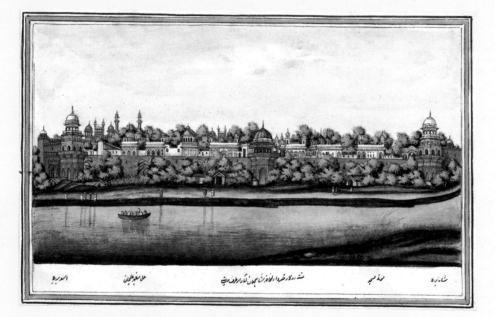

الدوربة   علامغیرطیلان   منشه روکار مقرره دار الخاور بنیان نگار دولن ونیه   مرة مسید   شانه بره

نقشه قدسیه باغ درکنت دلی جهانبها در

The Koodseea Bagh or Garden was constructed by the Newab
Koodseea Begum, mother of the Emperor Mohummud Shah,
during the reign of her son — Page 12 — and named after her
= self — It is situated immediately in the Environs and to
the North of the City — Formerly a splendid Palace, but now
much dilapidated and neglected — It belongs to the Heir
Apparent for the time being —

1. Pure — Chaste —

I do not think that any entertainments at any period of our lives gave us such enjoyment as did those on Gala Days. How joyously happy we were! Georgie and I always looked back with loving memories to those days.

The rules at Hill House were few and simple, but stringent:

To rise at 7 o'clock.	*Silence* in bedrooms
To be dressed by 7.30.	To pray and read Bibles until
Breakfast 8 o'clock,	afterwards prayers in drawing room.
Begin lessons at 9 o'clock.	Classes lasting only half an hour when we were small children, but afterwards lengthened.

An interval of ten minutes' relaxation between classes when we might talk – otherwise perfect silence.

Daily walk before dinner at 1 o'clock.

An hour in garden in afternoon.

Tea at 5 o'clock.	Prayers at 7.30.

Supper of cake – then bed at 8 when we were small – afterwards at 9 o'clock.

This was the simple daily régime of which we never tired, for it was a rule of loving kindness and happiness, although implicit obedience was expected.

The extract above is enough to make anyone grateful that they were not born in Victorian days. On the other hand, even such famous advocates of the "by all means spare the rod and spoil your child" school as Dr Spock seem to be coming round to the view that too much soft-heartedness and spoiling can be even worse than too little – or none at all. And although, looking back from these enlightened days, we may see a great many things that we find horrifying in the Victorian treatment of children, there is little doubt that a disciplined child is in general far happier than an undisciplined one, since the latter spends half its time in tears and tantrums – in order, presumably, to discover just how much nonsense its parents will stand for. Most Victorian children may have been in awe of their parents, and many may even have been frightened of them. But they certainly never despised them, as the twentieth-century child is apt to do. And, let's face it, when they grew up they went out and conquered half the world.

*M*rs Umphelby was assisted during the eight years I spent at Belstead by a very clever and well educated governess, Miss Bailey, whom we all called "Madame" as she had a French mother and had been brought up in France. She was a good linguist and a very accomplished artist, and was in fact a singularly capable and agreeable woman, with a high standard of education for *those* days – the forties of this last century.

That was, of course, a very different standard to what is now required in a first-class school.

Besides Miss Bailey there were occasional masters for different accomplishments, and Mrs Umphelby herself took the department of English education – history, literature, etc. – entirely into her own hands. She also taught the harp exceedingly well and Madame took the piano instruction. Everything worked like clockwork: no friction nor unpunctuality, and strict discipline, but in loving hands like Mrs Umphelby's there was no want or discomfort, and no punishments beyond the loss of a ticket for good conduct, and the knowledge of Mrs Umphelby's grieved displeasure.

The principal points as to conduct were notified by tickets given by Mrs Umphelby at the end of every week for "Truth", "Obedience", "Self Control" and "Attention to Studies". The possession of these – or the loss of them – were matters of infinite importance to us children.

The bestowing of "tickets" seems to have been a favourite Victorian ploy. My mother (who, as I write this, is two weeks short of her ninety-third birthday and still going strong) told me that when she was a child her family had two "cards" that were given for bad manners: the card to be worn hung around the neck of the recipient for a set space of time, unless someone else earned it before the deadline was up. Each bore the picture of a pig – one in black-and-white and the other in colour – the "Pig Card" being presented for minor transgressions and the "Illuminated Pig Card" for major ones. She also told me that on one famous occasion my grandmother, whose conversation at the breakfast table was not being attended to, remarked tartly: "Really, talking to you children is like casting pearls before . . ." At which point she stopped abruptly, and my grandfather solemnly presented her with the "Illuminated Pig Card".

Our mother having wished that we should be placed entirely under Mrs Umphelby's guardianship, we spent our holidays too with her, unless some of our relatives wished to have us for a few weeks. We were always happy at Belstead and satisfied with the simple pleasures of country life. The haymaking in summer was a great delight, and the long drives in the pretty country round Ipswich and picnics were always a great enjoyment to us. We each had a little bit of garden to dig in and grow flowers according to our own fancy, and an especial treat was to be taken by Mrs Umphelby for a shopping expedition to Ipswich, three miles off, in the pony-carriage. And on these occasions she would teach us to drive the Shetland pony, and we would have luncheon at the Pastrycook's and revel in potted meat sandwiches! Then on Sundays we all went to morning service at a church in Ipswich, driving there in large waggonettes with covers and curtains which could be closed against rain, wind or sun.

The services in St Helen's Church, Ipswich, were very dull for small children, and the sermons of the Rev J. Nottedge, a very intellectual and holy old man, were quite above our heads. But after his death we went to St Peter's Church where there was more singing and a much more interesting minister, the Rev Henry Lumsden, whom we all adored, and with whom we kept up an acquaintance as long as he lived.

In the long summer days we used to go to afternoon or evening service at Belstead Church, which was a hot, tiring walk of one and a half miles from Hill House. The church was a most antiquated building: small, with a gallery at one end in which the village orchestra used to play the hymn tunes on a set of very discordant instruments, and the singing was led by the clerk with a series of flourishes and twirligigs of his own invention that were more like a lunatic's proceedings than those of church music.

Surrounding the church was a quiet churchyard shaded by some fine trees, in which our dear friend Mrs Umphelby was to be laid to rest in 1887, in the same grave with her father and mother. I have a little watercolour of the church and of her grave which hangs below the picture of our dear Belstead home – both of which are to be my Emmie's, as I know she will treasure them.

During the summer holidays we frequently went with Mrs Umphelby to Languard Fort, about ten miles from Ipswich, on the East Coast at the mouth of the River Orwell. It had been built as a watch tower against invasion, and was greatly strengthened when there was a fear of Napoleon's sudden descent on that coast. It had ample accommodation for a considerable force of artillery and infantry, but when we went there, there were only a few gunners, a sergeant and a sergeant-major whose very robust, red-faced, brawny-armed wife used to dip us all into the sea twice a week.

It is worth remembering that at the time Emily is writing about more than half the population of Great Britain would remember the Napoleonic Wars, and a large number would actually have taken part in them, for Waterloo had been fought little more than twenty-five years before, Napoleon had been dead for about twenty, and the Duke of Wellington was still very much alive. Many of the Martello Towers – those small, fortified towers that were built to protect the south and southeast coast of England from invasion by Napoleon's army – still stand; the majority of them now privately owned and used as weekend or summer holiday homes, although some are still preserved as small fortresses. And not so long ago, when it was expected that Hitler would attempt an invasion, all these towers, together with Languard Fort and such ancient guardians of the English coast as Dover and Pevensey Castles, were made ready to play their original rôles again.

*T*he Governor of the fort was Colonel West, a friend of Mrs Umphelby's – who seldom visited the fort – and was allowed to lend the "Governor's House" to friends for short periods, so we visited the fort several years in succession, thoroughly enjoying the novelty of the place and also the charming gardens laid out between the fort and the River Orwell.

We used always to drive there, passing through the village of Felixstowe – then a quiet village but now a fashionable watering-place. The sea has made considerable encroachments on that coast, and Sir Samuel Dickens' house and grounds, which formerly adorned the village of Felixstowe, have now been entirely washed away from their position near the beach. A beautiful sandy beach it always was, but whether it still preserves that character I do not know.

From Languard Fort we saw, two years at least, the Royal Squadron passing up to Scotland with the Queen and Prince Albert and their family on board – although of course at too great a distance to distinguish persons. But a Royal Salute was fired when the vessels passed in the distance, and there was great excitement among us as we watched these proceedings from the ramparts of the fort.

We spent the Christmas holidays of 1842 at Deer Park, Honiton, with Aunt Smythe, who was then keeping house for our uncle, Sir Charles Metcalfe, and I used to get many rides on horseback with old Uncle Smythe, who was always very kind to me. We went for long rides through very lovely country, which I thoroughly enjoyed. Of course we were still quite small children in the school-room with our cousin Emily Smythe, and we all had great fun together.

Uncle Charles had returned from Jamaica where he had been Governor since 1838, and was suffering from swelling and wounds in his face which caused him much pain. But when called to duty again as Governor-General of Canada he would not refuse, and went out there in 1843. He suffered very acutely for two years, when he was obliged to give up his office and return to England in 1845, where he was made a peer. He continued to suffer terribly from cancer in his face until he died in September 1846, at Matchanger, near Basingstoke.

In 1841 our sister Eliza came home from India under the care of our old Nurse, Phoebe Saunders, and came to Belstead to be brought up with Georgie and me. But the winter of the following year, 1842, was a very sad time for all of us, as on November 20th our aunt, Mrs George Lawrence, and dear Grandmama Browne came down suddenly to Belstead to bring us the sorrowful tidings that our precious Mother had died in India, at Simla, on September 26th of that year.

They brought us a letter from dear Daddy about her death, and although so many years have passed since then the events of that day and the great sorrow that came to our young hearts are as fresh now as ever. For we remembered our dear Mother and our love for her had been cherished by Mrs Umphelby. The correspondence between us had been constant, and we had always been told what a rare being she was in every way, so that it was a *real* sorrow, even though we were so young.

We did not see as much of our brother Theo as we should have done. He was under Mrs Smythe's care, and she kept him too much at his school, even in the holidays, as he was troublesome at home without companions, so he had not a happy childhood. But he much enjoyed himself at Languard Fort with us in the Summer holidays of 1844 – the last we spent there.

In 1845 we spent the Summer holidays with Aunt Smythe at Tunbridge Wells and enjoyed ourselves greatly. Our youngest brother Charlie had come home that Spring, and was sent to Aunt Smythe's care also. He was a very fine boy; fascinating, but a little scamp in many ways, and gave his sisters a great deal of trouble. We had delightful drives to Penshurst, Knoll and Bayham Abbey. The three mansions and parks I have remembered with pleasure all my life as so full of interesting historical associations, as well as magnificent buildings and abodes of luxury and comfort and beauty.

Aunt Mary, who had married Edward Colvin a few years previously and been out in India, had brought Charlie home, and both having lately been in Delhi with my Father they were able to tell us a great deal of his life and much that was interesting to us. Aunt Mary had also brought home our Mother's jewellery, and this, as arranged by Father himself before he sent it, was divided into three parts.

Of course we all prized it exceedingly, but my sister Eliza afterwards imagined she had less than she ought to have had in the division, and was jealous over it, although I have a letter from my Father saying he had arranged it as fairly as he could. Eli therefore had no cause for complaint. But she sold or exchanged the jewellery allotted to her for articles she preferred, whereas I have kept mine to this day, although the stones in some cases are mounted differently. Many articles have been given away to my daughters and all are dearly prized; but my Mother had not much jewellery, except some fine pearls which were stolen soon after her death in India – to my dear Father's great annoyance, though carefully guarded by three Chubbs' locks in a strong box. 🙖

How many families – or how few – have not squabbled over the division of property left by a deceased relative? One hears of it only too often, and we cannot be too sure that "Eli" did not have some cause for complaint, because her father's delightful "Dehlie Book" was compiled by him "For My Very Dear Girls, from their affectionate Father". Yet, written on the first page, added later and in a hand that does not look like Sir Thomas' (perhaps a handwriting expert could tell us?) is: "Emily Annie Theophila Bayley. Her Father's Gift".

Could it be that Emily wrote this herself in order that there should be no doubt as to who had the book? It would be interesting to know. Although, as the eldest of the "Very Dear Girls", she could of course have claimed it on the grounds of seniority, and it would certainly have been a crying shame if it had been divided up and a few pages of it given to each daughter; so if she did one can only say, "Well done!"

We spent a very happy Christmas holiday in 1845–46 with my dear Aunt and Uncle Colvin, who were living in a fine house in Manchester Street with old Mr Colvin, his delightful father, and his daughter Margaret Colvin, a very charming woman, both of whom were so good as to have we three children for five weeks in their house. We were very happy and enjoyed ourselves tremendously, having plenty of young friends in different branches of the Colvin family.

It was during this winter that my brother Theo was laid up in London, suffering great pain in his eyes which ended in the terrible affliction of total blindness in his right eye – a trial which threw a cloud over his life. He was at Addiscombe, the Military Academy of the East India Company, preparing for a cadetship in the Indian Army, and was seventeen and a very handsome, promising boy. He bore the suffering from violent inflammation with great courage and patience, as also the destruction of all his ardent hopes of a military career, which were of course entirely destroyed. But kind friends in the India Office interested themselves on his account and procured 🙖

him a civil appointment to India, so he went to Haileybury College in 1847, spent two years there, and went out to India in 1849. ❧

"The Honourable Company of Merchants of London trading to the East Indies" – "John Company" – who in those pre-Mutiny days held power in India, had their own College, Addiscombe, where boys who wished to enter the Company's service, either in a civilian capacity or as an officer in the "Bengal Army", the Company's sepoy army, were sent to be educated. The writer Sir John Kaye, his brother Edward and their first cousin, William, who was my grandfather, all went to Addiscombe, and I still have my grandfather's passing-out certificate. But after the Mutiny the Company's charter was not renewed, and the Government of India was taken over by the Crown. Addiscombe merged with Haileybury, and is now just one of a number of well known British public schools.

*I*n the Spring of 1846 my studies were energetically prosecuted and extra lessons from London masters in music gave me both pleasure and great benefit. The Summer holidays were spent at Bonchurch in the Isle of Wight, where Mrs Umphelby had taken a charming house, and in June a great event in my life took place – being bridesmaid to my cousin Charlotte Flower, who was married to the Duke of Marlborough at Lambeth Palace by the Archbishop of Canterbury, Dr Howley.

It was my first peep into Society life, and I greatly enjoyed this unusual event in my quiet country-school existence. Besides I was especially fond of this cousin, and both Emily Smythe and I joined a very handsome group of ten bridesmaids – all much older than us. Our dresses were simple, but very pretty: white muslin trimmed with real Valenciennes on the bodices, pink gauze scarves and pink chiffon hats. The Wedding Breakfast was at No. 1 Chesham Place, and we were allowed to stand in the balcony and watch all the guests arriving and departing. All the splendid presents were exhibited, and as I had never seen such beautiful things I was struck with wonder and admiration. The Duke was a good deal older than my cousin, but a very handsome man, and extremely kind to me. But although their first years were *very happy*, the marriage was not happy to the end, despite her loving him dearly. ❧

Among other enjoyments this year was a visit to Blenheim to stay with the bride, which I enjoyed most thoroughly, as I received the greatest kindness from Charlotte and her husband, and was charmed with everything I saw. It was all indelibly impressed on my mind, for when I paid another visit to Blenheim in 1902, merely as a sightseer, I found that I recollected everything quite accurately, and noted all the alterations that had taken place; to the astonishment of the old servants who had been there many years. Especially did I ask to see a little room that opened on to the rose garden where we always dined on Sundays.

It was a beautiful spot, but when I said to the guide, "I should like to see that room again," she said, "Oh! *do* you remember it? It has been turned into the Secretary's room, and is not shown to visitors."

In going through the superb rooms that are full of beautiful things, I was looking for a marble bust of my cousin Charlotte, which I knew had been executed after her death. But the guide could not tell me where it was until I found it on a side table in a room seldom used, and the guide was much surprised at being told who it was, for although he had been there many years he had never been able to find out. The magnificent library had been despoiled of its valuable books, sold to pay the debts of the duke who succeeded my cousin's husband in possession. In recent years it had been turned into a music room, where a most beautiful organ was played daily for the benefit of visitors. This was done by the young American lady who became duchess, but who had a very unhappy life, her only happiness being in her two sons. [*The "young American lady" was the beautiful Consuelo Vanderbilt whose autobiography,* The Glitter and the Gold, *gives an account of her life at Blenheim and elsewhere, and whose grandson is the present Duke of Marlborough.* MMK]

It was sad going over the place where I had been so happy, and I could still recognize my old bedroom window, recalling many happy memories of the time when my dear cousin was alive.

I had been at Hill House since 1840, the year I first went there with my sister Georgie (Lady Campbell) and it was a blessed home to both of us: to Georgie for ten years and to me for seven. But in 1847, my Father having expressed a wish that I should go out to India in the care of my aunt and uncle, Mr and Mrs Edward Colvin, it was decided that I was to leave with them that Autumn, and we sailed from Southampton in the steamer *Indus* on October 20th of that year; less than eight weeks after my seventeenth birthday.

Mrs Umphelby and Theo travelled with me to see me off, and it was a very sad parting. I felt it deeply for I was leaving my darling Georgie, from whom I had never been parted before, as well as my happy home at Belstead. But from the commencement of the voyage Uncle Edward showed me the utmost sympathy and tenderness, and throughout the next ten years until he died in 1857 he was my truest, kindest and best friend, while dear Aunt Mary was like a tender mother to me throughout the remainder of her life.

I knew nobody on board ship when I started, but as the Colvins knew several of the passengers we had a pleasant circle of acquaintances. Mrs Macdonald, Mrs Tierney, Mr and Mrs Dalrymple, Major Charles Havelock and Captain Read of the Fourteenth Hussars. To these were soon added Mr and Mrs George Macintosh, who on discovering my name at once claimed friendship, she being the daughter of Mr Gardner, one of the oldest friends of the Metcalfe family. She was then quite young, like myself, and throughout life has always been a true friend to me.

We had a rough passage in the English Channel and through the Bay of Biscay, and one of my strongest memories is watching the Isle of Wight fading away in the distance and wondering if ever I should see it again.

Our first halt was at Gibraltar, and as it was also my first experience of foreign life I was enchanted with all I saw that day: the luxuriant abundance of fruit in the market, and the gay, picturesque dresses of the people. It is still as fresh in my memory, forty-seven years afterwards, as if it were yesterday, although I have never seen the place again.

A day spent at Valetta, in Malta, was equally full of enjoyment, and our drive to Citta Vecchia and a visit to the Catacombs and to St John's Armoury were sources of great pleasure. Our next halt was at Alexandria where we left the *Indus*, and after a few hours wandering about the town had to board a steam-barge and travel all night up the Mahmoudieh Canal to Cairo. [*There was no Suez Canal at that time, and the day that the first ships would pass through it still lay twenty years ahead.* MMK]

The boat was densely crowded with passengers, and of course all the snug berths were given over to the elderly members of the party, the younger ones having to sleep on the floor or wherever they could find a resting-place.

We arrived at Boulac on the canal before daylight, and were then driven in omnibuses to Shepherd's Hotel at Cairo, preceded by Arabs running with flaming torches. The hotel was already over-flowing with passengers from India who had reached it before we did, so again no beds were available and the elder members of the party laid down on the couches in the public rooms, but we younger members decided to have baths, and were escorted by Arabs through narrow lanes to some establishment where we could get them.

We all enjoyed the fun and excitement of walking about an eastern town at night, escorted by several Arab servants with their torches, and having had our baths we were quite ready for coffee and bread and butter when we returned to the hotel. But everything was so new, so delightful and so strange, that of course we were in no mood to go to sleep, and sat on the steps of the hotel until the early morning, watching the gathering together of the donkeys and donkey-boys, and interested by all the strange sights that Cairo presented to us, for in those days it was nothing but an oriental town, with no veneer of European customs.

There was then no railroad in Egypt, and the mode of progression across the desert from Cairo to Suez was by small, covered vans drawn by four horses that had been scarcely broken in at all, and driven at a tremendous pace by Arab drivers armed with long whips. I forget how many vans were needed to accommodate all the passengers from the *Indus*, but each held six people, and our party, which consisted of my uncle and aunt, our friends Mrs Macdonald and Mrs Tierney, myself and Major Charles Havelock, packed ourselves into one that evening to be driven to Suez during the night.

It was a most uncomfortable conveyance, and the journey, for those who were not strong, a most trying one. But in those days everything was delightful to me. I was as happy as a bird, and thoroughly enjoyed every moment of my life, even the many discomforts of travel.

In one of my novels, *Shadow of the Moon*, I sent a handful of my characters to Suez in one of these desert vans – which must have been among the most uncomfortable vehicles ever invented. But, as Emily has pointed out, there were no railways in Egypt at that time (or in India either) and, since there was no Suez Canal, travellers had to choose between a long voyage round the Cape and up the east coast of Africa, or taking a ship as far as Alexandria, disembarking themselves and their luggage there, and going on, *via* Cairo and the desert, to Suez, where they would board another boat – a P & O or an "East Indiaman", which would take them down the Red Sea to Aden, and on to India. Incidentally, when the Suez Canal was formally declared open, twenty years later, it was Emily's old school-friend, Eugénie, who graced that ceremony with her presence as Empress of the French.

*T*here were three halts made on the way to Suez, the drive occupying from seventeen to eighteen hours, across the desert. The caravanserais, or rest-houses, were large enclosures, built of sand and mud, in which there were one or two large rooms (quite bare of furniture except for tables and chairs) where tea and rough meals were provided for the passengers; and there were smaller rooms where the travellers were expected to arrange their dress on the journey. Everything was in the roughest style. In the stables attached to these caravanserais were relays of horses for the vans, and about ten of these cars started together at the same hour, followed at the space of three hours later by another set, and again three hours later by a third, according to the amount of accommodation required.

It was a headlong gallop the whole way across the desert, where there was no regular road but only a beaten track along which the cars were in the habit of passing, and as the horses were very wild and often swerved off this track, it was no wonder that in the darkness of the night, going at a furious pace, accidents occasionally happened.

Such was our experience, for in the dead of the night, when we were all dozing (or trying to doze despite the shaking and creaking of the carriage) we felt a tremendous shock, and the carriage was overturned. We had gone over a large boulder, and come down with a tremendous smash.

Three of the occupants of the car were lying on their backs on the ground, and the other three, of whom I was one, were either thrown on the top of them or thrown out of the door. The Arab drivers rushed after their horses, which had got loose, and we had to attend to ourselves as best we could. Major Havelock was fortunately thrown out at the door, and having sustained no injury, he helped to get me out next, then Mrs Macdonald, and finally Mrs Tierney and my uncle and aunt. All were terribly shaken, but no one except myself had received any injury apart from bruises and shock. I had got a very bad blow over my left eye, and for many days afterwards had to wear a bandage over it.

It was an awkward predicament to find ourselves stranded in the desert in the middle of a dark night, but fortunately another van full of passengers came up just as we were beginning to wonder what we should do, and how we were to get on, as one of the wheels was smashed. We then found we were close to one of the caravanserais, where we could get food and rest for some hours.

The beautiful starlit night enabled us to reach it without difficulty, so we all walked to it, and remained there until breakfast-time next morning, when we started in a fresh van, and finally, accompanied by the other passengers, reached Suez by midday where we were glad to find ourselves in a large hotel, and to get some tolerable food – roast pigeons and macaroni. The hotel was kept by a Frenchman, and although very eastern in its arrangements had some comfortable bedrooms in which we were able to get to sleep that night. [*The nationality of the proprietor probably accounts for the fact that, in spite of describing the meal as merely "tolerable", Emily can remember, 47 years later, exactly what she ate! –* MMK] The air of Suez struck me then, as it has done each time, as being so fresh and light and delightful – which was just as well, as we had to remain there until the rest of the passengers came up from Cairo, and the P & O steamer from India arrived to take us all on. This it did two days later, and a boatful of Anglo-Indian passengers took over the hotel while we went on board and occupied the cabins they had vacated.

In those days – and well into my own! – "Anglo-Indian" did not mean, as it does now, a person of mixed blood, but any of the British who were in the service of the Government of India, or who, for trade or any other purpose, were resident in that country for the term of their working lives.

There is a poem in Kipling's *Just So Stories* that begins "China-going

P & Os . . .". To those who do not remember the P & Os, the magic letters stand for "Peninsular and Oriental". And apart from going on to China, the ships of that line carried generations of men and women to and fro between England and India, year after year. In another poem Kipling calls it the "Exiles Line" – "The Exiles' Line brings out the exiles' line, And ships them homeward when their work is done" . . . and the final verse ends: "For all the soul of our sad East is there, Beneath the house-flag of the P & O." The flocks of girls who arrived in India at the beginning of each year came to be known as the "Fishing Fleet", while those who sailed away again, unwed or unengaged, were known more cruelly as "Returned Empties". But to thousands of people the P & O stood for adventure, romance and the magic spell of the East, even though to others it meant only hard work or hard fighting, and exile.

For a time, after India achieved Independence, the liners still sailed from Southampton or Liverpool to Karachi, Bombay, Ceylon, Madras, Calcutta . . . and on eastward to Rangoon and Penang, Singapore, Hong Kong and Shanghai . . . But there were fewer and fewer passengers. The Raj had ended and the Air Age had begun, and P & Os, like the dinosaurs, became extinct (the company, of course, is still in existence). Yet as long as anyone who served in the India-of-the-Raj remains alive, they will live on in fond memory.

*T*he cabins proved to be most primitive arrangements, but we were young and happy (at least a good many of the party were) and we soon forgot our troubles – except myself, who still had a very bad black eye from the blow I had received when the desert-van upset, and which only got well just as we reached Calcutta three weeks later.

We had an uneventful voyage down to Aden, where we arrived after six days' steaming, late one evening. By the time we disembarked it was a glorious moonlit night, and I shall never forget our stroll along the sea shore, such a bright, merry party, with Mrs Cochrane, another of our steamer friends, a buoyant Irish girl, leading all the fun. Such a horrid-looking place Aden was, the tall, black, rocky cliffs, the black roads and the black figures dancing about in the moonlight making a most weird scene altogether, and we were quite ready to believe the legend that a curse rests on it as being Cain's burial-place.

I have never heard this legend associated with Aden before; although I imagine it crops up in many grim and desolate-looking places. Kabul, the capital of Afghanistan, is supposed to have been founded by Cain, whose bones, so it is said, lie buried under a hill to the south of the city. I suppose Aden could be described as "forbidding", for it is an arid and rocky place. But it certainly never seemed so to me; probably because my memories of it are daytime ones: "The barren rocks of Aden" in the dawn, with the rising sun turning their heights to a bright gold reflected in an opal sea. A pale, shimmering, blue-grey in the heat of midday, or rose pink and cerise with deep blue shadows as one sailed away from it at sunset. And, like Emily, uncounted travellers must have gone ashore there with their friends, and been as merry as she was.

*T*he ladies of our party managed to get four or five beds standing in a row in a verandah enclosed by mats, and fortunately we had mosquito curtains with us, so that we were able to lie down, but not to sleep, for the rats jumped over our beds and kept us wide awake; but we were all very merry and enjoyed the fun of such novel experiences.

The next morning the steamer left early, and we had a pleasant voyage to Pointe de Galle. There the impression made on my mind was one of intense admiration for everything in Ceylon, and each time that I have visited it this feeling has been strengthened. Everything was so new as regards the people and the houses, and so beautiful were the trees, and shrubs, and flowers, that I looked upon it as a kind of paradise.

No one, then or now, could fail to be enchanted by the beauty of Ceylon – or Sri Lanka as it is now called. That wet, green, lovely island must surely be one of the most beautiful places in this beautiful world, for it seems to have everything: tree-clad hills and crystal-clear seas, white sandy beaches, a colourful profusion of flowers, and rank upon rank of coconut palms bending to the sea wind as though waving a greeting to arriving travellers, or a farewell to those who are leaving.

By contrast, Madras, Emily's next stop, when seen from the deck of a ship is a flat and uninteresting place: white houses and a long line of white breakers crashing onto a shore that seems to stretch for miles. But once when we landed there the docks and the sea front were made incredibly beautiful by thousands of huge black and scarlet butterflies, lilting and floating through the hot sunlight.

We were there only during the day, and did not sleep on shore, for the steamer started again early the next morning. Our next halt was off the coast of Madras, and owing to the very heavy sea that was running there was great difficulty in landing both passengers and luggage. There was great excitement and amusement in watching the native boats and catamarans that came off through the boiling surf to the ships, but the sight was a grotesque one, with none of the beauty and charm of what we had seen in Ceylon. The men in the boats were quite naked except for a strip of cloth round their loins, and their yells and jabberings were ludicrous to the ear.

My friend Mrs Cochrane went on shore here and I never saw her again, although we corresponded with her for many years afterwards.

The excitement was great as the steamer neared Calcutta, because we had to pass the dangerous sandbank, the James and Mary, on which many fine vessels had been stranded and sucked down by the peculiar nature of the quicksands, most of the passengers losing their lives. It is still a great danger, and there are so many stories of ships that have been lost on it, that captains of vessels are nervous and anxious till they have passed without touching it, and we were all thankful when we were safely out of its reach. 🐾

Emily does not mention that then, as now, ships bound for the port of Calcutta must anchor off the "Sandheads" at the mouth of the Hooghly River, to wait for the tide and to take a pilot on board. For of all navigable rivers, the Hooghly is the most dangerous, because of the many shoals and sandbanks that lie hidden under its swirling, silt-laden water, and which are forever shifting and changing at the whim of the treacherous currents. The most notorious of these sandbanks is the deadly James and Mary, whose quicksands have become the graveyard of countless ships, and which takes its name from one of its victims, the *Royal James and Mary*, wrecked there in 1694. Once aground on it no ship can hope to escape; and buoys are useless, because of the swiftness with which the bank can change

Continued on page 113

The Zeenut-ool-Musajid or Ornament Mosque was erected by the Zeenut ool Nissa, a Daughter of the Emperor Aurung=zebe who reigned between the Years 1659 and 1707 A.D. of our Era. It is of red Stone with enlayings of Marble with a spaci=ous Terrace in front, and a Capaceous Reservoir faced with Marble. It is considerably elevated and stands close to the River Gate of the City.

The Royal Founder having determined on a life of Celebacy, laid out a large Sum of money in the above Mosque, and on its completeon she constructed a Sepulchre of white marble surrounded by a Wall of the same costly material on the West Evenue of the Terrace. Here she was buried A.D. 1710. Formerly lands yielding an annual Revenue of 100,000 Rs = 10,000 £ of our money, were allotted for the Support of the Priests and Servants and the Repairs of the Building, but they have long since been alienated.

One of the principal objects after entering the Palace, that attracts attention, is the Dewan e aum, or Public Hall of Audience for all descriptions of Persons. It is situated at the upper end of a spacious Square and though at present much neglected is still a noble Building. The length is 196 feet and Breadth 64 feet. The Roof is supported by a succession of flat arches of Red Stone on Pillars of the same Material, but now disfigured by the bad taste of Modern times with a Coating of white Plaister - On each side of the Hall and all round the Square are Arcades which are said in former Days of Splendor to have been adorned with the richest Tapestry. But in these degenerate times, the Walls are bare, and the buildings themselves used as Stables or Lumber rooms.

In the Interior of the Dewan e aum, is a Massive Marble Throne handsomely carved and below it a large Slab of the same Material on which, on public Days, the chief Ministers took their stand and handed up Petitions to the Emperor. This slab was beautifully inlaid with Mosaic Work, all of which has been removed.

In a recess in the rear of the Throne is a gilt door way, through which the Emperor entered. The Recess is ornamented with Mosaic Work of the most exquisite Workmanship, and of which several Specimens will be found in the succeeding pages.

The Dewan e aum is now never appropriated to its original purpose and indeed is nothing more than a receptacle for all kinds of Rubbish. Shame to the Ruling Power, whether it be the King as immediate or the British Government as Lord Paramount.

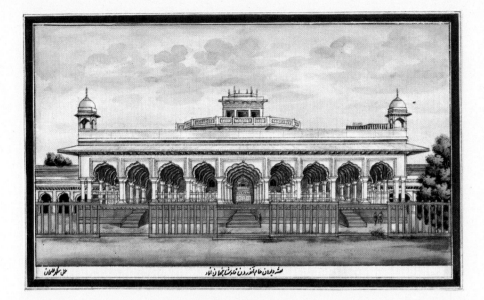

نقشهٔ دیوان عام از درون قلعهٔ شاه جهان آباد ناظر

علی سفیر طهران

نقشهٔ کرسی اندرونی دیوان عام سلطنت

علی سفیر طهران

In the Royal Garden to the North of the Dewan e Khass or Hall of Audience is a large Octagon Tower lined with Marble and called the Shah Boorj or Royal Tower. It faces the River Jumna and from this Tower, the then Heir Apparent Prince Mirza Jewwun Bukht, eldest Son of the unfortunate Emperor Shah Aulum, made his Escape in 1784. He threw himself from the projecting Parapet into the River and haveing succeeded in gaining the opposite bank, fled to Lucknow.

The Descendants of this Prince are now settled at Benares. Beneath this Tower, the celebrated Canal excavated by Ullee Murdan Khan, a nobleman of the Court of the Emperor Shah-e Juhan, enters the Palace Garden through a small aperture, and falling over a large Marble Slab formerly inlaid with flowers delineated in Cornelian of different Colours, takes its way through Marble Channels to the interior Apartments.

Within the Tower is the beautiful fountain as shown below of light green Agate, surrounded with Mosaic work – Certainly the most Chaste and unique Specimen of the kind now Known – but at the present time most sadly neglected.

صفہ میناہ مسجد الورون قلعہ شاہجہان آباد

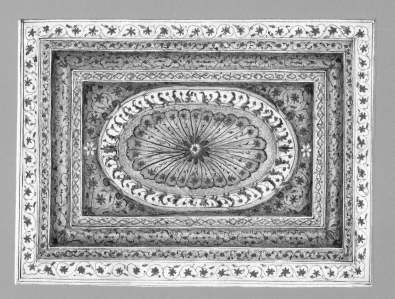

The Soneiree Musjid or Golden Mosque, so denominated from its gilt Domes is situated within the city and nearly opposite the Palace. It was constructed in A.D. 1747, by the Nawab Buhadur Khan, a Nobleman of the Reign of the Emperor Ahmed Shah, and is built of the Bassee-Sung or a light Salmon coloured Stone not usually applied to this purpose, which gives the building a Singular and Picturesque Appearance.

The Natives of India though willing to erect Expensive Edifices in order to perpetuate their own Names, are not equally liberal in repairing the public works of their Predecessors.

The Nawab Ahmed Bukhsh Khan, father of the wretched Nawab of Ferozepoor, was an exception to this Rule, for he repaired the Mosque in question with a View to the benefit of the Neighborhood. Soon after when passing by with his Second and favorite Son, he was attacked by an infuriated Elephant, who killed one of the Horses and dashed the Vehicle to pieces

The Nawab and his Son were only saved from Destruction by the proximity of this Mosque in which they were able to take Refuge.

This incident has added not a little to the Interest of the Building.

† Known in History also by the name of Javeid who supplanted the Nawab Sefder Jung (see page 24) the Minister in the good opinion of the Emperor Ahmed Shah. In revenge, the Nawab invited Javeid to an Entertainment and caused him to be murdered during the Banquet.

The Molee Musjid or Pearl Mosque within the precincts of the Royal Palace is entirely of Marble. It was constructed by the Emperor Aurungzeb Aulumgeer, literally the ornament of the Throne and Conqueror of the World, who reigned between the Years A.D. 1658 and 1707.

Its origin is attributed to a fit of Compunction for the Cruelties exercised by him towards his two elder brothers Dara Shekoh and Moorad.

It is a very beautiful Mosque, but from being enclosed in the front and both sides by high Walls, is not seen to advantage.

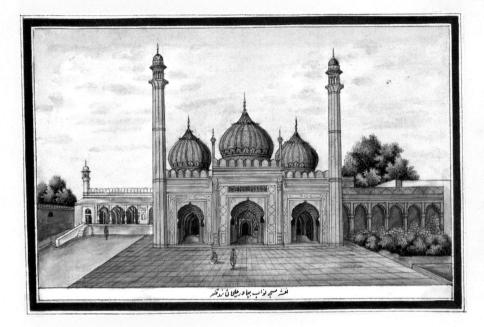

نقشہ مسجد نواب بہادر علیخاں زدقلعہ

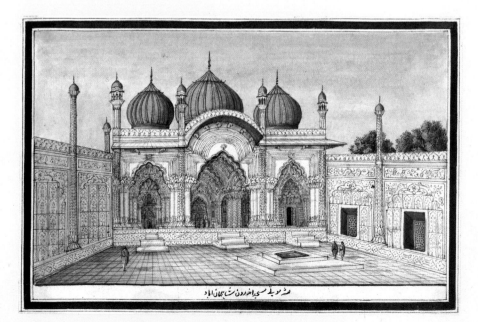

نقشہ موتی مسجد اندرون شہجہان آباد

The Shrine of the Celebrated Saint Nizamoodeen (the regulator of the Faith) is situated to the S.S.E. from Dehly distant about a mile from the Mausoleum of the Emperor Hoomaioon the Propitious. see page 9. Nizamoodeen who was also entitled The Prince of Holy men. The Saint. The Magnificent. The Munificent and the beloved of God, was born at Ghuznee in Afghanistan, about the year A.D. 1237, provided the date of the Mahomedan Æra be correct Viz. in 635, of the Hegirah or year of the flight of the Prophet Mahomet. The progenitors of Nizamoodeen were natives of Bokhara. When young the Subject of this Memoir appears to have accompanied his father to Hindoostan, and to have resided for some time at Budaoon in Rohilkhund: but at an early age, native historians say 20, being already eminent for his Scientific and Theological attainments he resigned all secular pursuits and retired to the town of Ujoodhun in the Province of Mooltan. Having perfected himself as a disciple of a very Eminent Seer and devotee then residing in that Country. Nizamoodeen returned to Dehly after a lapse of 18 Years and according to oriental tradition, witnessed the Reigns of Seven Monarchs.

#	Meaning	#	Monarch	Year
1	Dear to Religion	1	Moizoodeen Kaikobad	A.D. 1286
2	Glory of Religion	2	Jullaloodeen 3 Khiljee	" 1288
3	Name of Tribe	4	Alaoodeen Khiljee	" 1295.
4	Glory of the Faith			
5	Pole Star or Pillar of the Faith	5	Kootooboodeen Mobaruck Shah	" 1357.
6	Prosperous 7 a King			"
8	Fair faced 9 Lord	8	Khosro Khan	" 1321.
10	Aid of Religion 11 Proper name	10	Ghiasoodeen Toghluck	" 1321.
12	a King - 13 the name of the	12	Sooltan Mohummed Shah	" 1325

Prophet. literally. Praised

It is related that the Emperor Ghiasoodeen Toghluck when returning from Bengal declared that on his arrival at Dehly he would cause Nizamoodeen to be ejected from the Imperial City, on which Nizamoodeen replied "Hunoz Dehly door ust". or yet Dehly is far distant. and it so happened that on approaching the Capital, the Emperor was met by his eldest Son Joona Khan who received him with Magnificence in a wooden
14 Ancient Lord } Pavilion erected for the occasion - During the ceremonies the Building gave
15 friendly Lord } way and crushed the Monarch with few other persons - This Misfortune may have been accidental, but the unusualness of erecting such a Structure at all, the opportune absence of the eldest Prince at the moment and the circumstance of the 2d. and favorite Son being involved in the same Calamity with the father, fixed strong suspicions on the Heir Apparent. The Mosque and large Baolee or Reservoir contiguous to the Shrine was built by Nizamoodeen himself. His Tomb which is visited by all religious Devotees, Hindoos as well as Mahomedans was erected by some of his disciples: but in the Reign of the Emperor Shahe Juhan - Khuleeboolla Khan a noble of the State, not only Embellished this much revered Shrine, but constructed the Buildings annexed thereto.

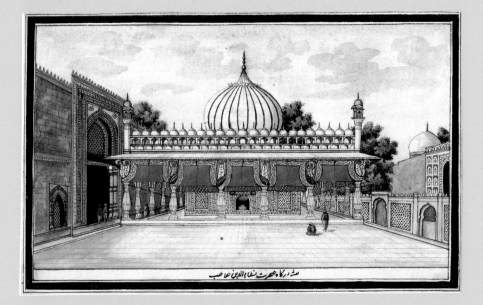

مشہد درگاہ حضرت نظام الدین صاحب

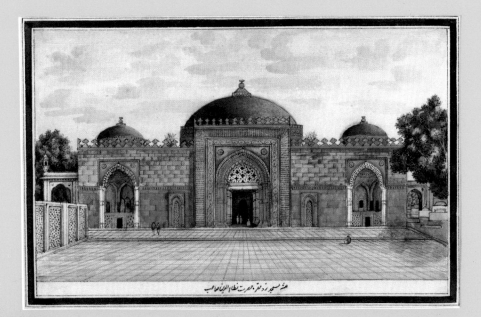

صفہ مسجد مزد دلقر حضرت نظام الدین صاحب

Within the enclosure of Nizamodeen's Tomb are the annexed Cenotophs, both of Marble and though executed at very different periods, they are both exquisite Specimens of Oriental designs and perfect Execution.

The one is sacred to the Memory of the unfortunate Emperor Mo-hummed Shah, referred to in Page 12. The lattice work of the Screen is is incomparable and the Massive Slab of which the Door way is composed most beautifully carved.

The Second is of much Modern date, though equally to be admired, having been erected in the Year 1821, to the Memory of the Prince Jehangeer (the Conquer-er of the World) the 4th Son of late Emperor Akber Shah.

This dissipated and turbulent Sicon of the Royal House evinced all the Characteristics, had he but possessed the Power of a 2d Absalom, and yet strange to say of all the Sons, he was the most cherished. Like also to the great Aurungzeb, he endeavored to supplant his elder brother and Strongly encouraged and Supported by his Father, he would, but from the protecting arm of the British Government, in all human probability have succeeded.

As it was in the year 1809, he created a serious Disturbance within the Palace, in the hope, that during this confusion, the destruction not only of the hated brother but the unsuspecting father might have en-sured his own Aggrandizement. Stringent measures were now deem-ed necessary to prevent more serious consequences; and the Rebellious Prince was banished to the Fortress of Allahabad (the City of God) where he remained a State Prisoner until in 1820, he closed a life of the grossest intemperance. His Remains were transferred to Dehly and here deposited.

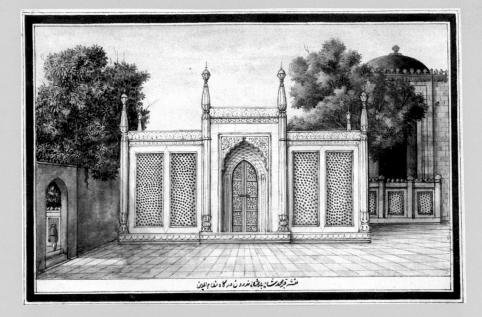

نقشۂ قبر محمد شاه پادشاه مغفور در درگاه نظام الدین

نقشۂ مقبرۂ جهانگیرزما ده در نظام الدین

علی ظفر الطان

The Chounsut Khumba or The Sixty four Pillars

A Marble Edifice adjoining to the Shrine of the Saint Nizamoodeen (the Expounder of the Faith) vide Page 40 was built by Meerza Uzeez Kokal Taush Khan the Son of Mohummud Shumsooddeen Khan, the husband of the wet nurse of the Emperor Mohummud Julal ooddeen Ukber, who was raised to the Rank of Nobility by the Title of Uzim Khan, During the reign of that Monarch and assassinated by one Ibraheem Udhum Khan, also foster brother to the Emperor, from a feeling of Envy on account of the Rank bestowed upon Shumsooddeen.

The Madman also attempted the life of the Emperor, but being rendered

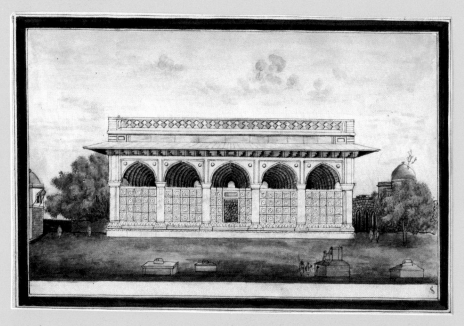

insensible by a blow from the Royal Fist, he was bound hand and foot and thrown over the Walls of the Palace.

He was buried near the Kootoob (Vide Page 74.) and an Edifice erected over his remains by his Mother, called Udhum ke Toombee or the Dome of Udhum –

The Remains of Mohummud Shumsooddeen Khan were interred in the Neighborhood of the Shrine of the Saint Nizam ooddeen and a suitable Tomb of Marble erected over them. Vide Drawing Page

The Emperor Commisserating Meerza Uzeez, the son of the deceased subsequently denominated him his own Son, and conferred on him the same Titles and Rank borne by his father. By this Individual was the Chounsut Khumba erected, & as a receptacle for his own Remains & here he was buried in the 19th Year of the Reign of the Emperor Juhangeer (Conqueror of the world) Son of the Emperor Ukbur, about the Year A.D: 1623.

---

1 Beloved
2 Kokal. foster Brother – Taeuk Personal, and in this Case Royal
3 Lord
4 Literally. Praised
5 Sun of Religion

6 Glory of Religion
7 the Heat.
8 the Chief
9 Abraham.
10. A name, without any particular meaning.

Another View of the same Building.

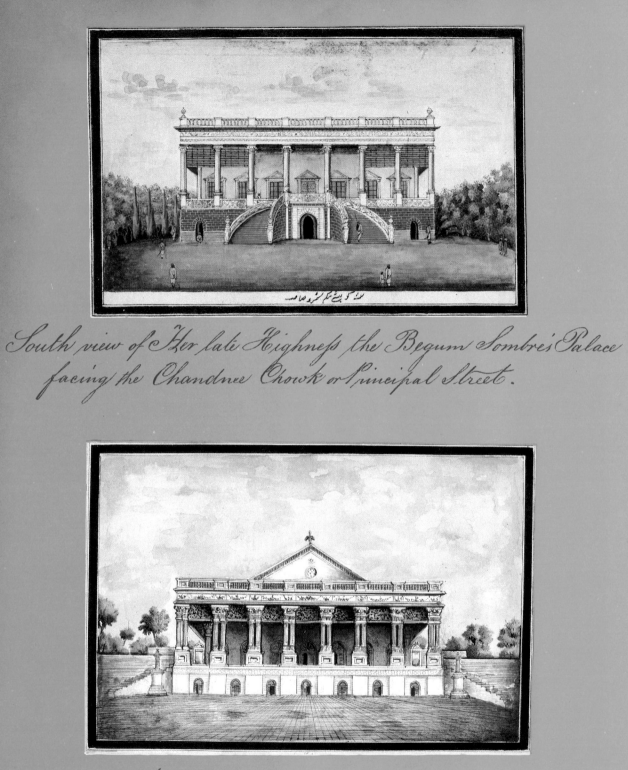

South view of Her late Highness the Begum Sombre's Palace
facing the Chandnee Chowk or Principal Street.

North view of the above.

The Begum Sombre was the widow of Walter Reinihard born of obscure parents in the Electorate of Treves, from whence he entered early into the French Service assuming the name of Summer, but from the darkness of his complexion he received the Sobriquet of Sombre subsequently corrupted into Sumroo, by which name Her Highness was generally known, though she always styled herself the Begum Sombre —

Sumroo soon after his enlistment in the French Service came to Bengal. Entered a Swiss Corps in Calcutta from which he deserted in 15 days. fled to the Upper Provinces and served for some time, as a private Trooper in the Cavalry of Sufdur Jung — Page 24. This service he also quitted and became attached to the Service of the Nabob of Bengal, in which Station he massacred the English Captives at Patna in 1763 — He again deserted from the Newab. served successively the Principal Chiefs of the time and died in 1776 —

The Begum's origin is involved in doubt — By some she is supposed to have been of a good Moghul Family, by others a native of Cashmere and to have been sold to Sombre as a Slave — She was of slight stature. of fair Complexion — distinguished by abilities of no common order and a daring seldom possessed by her Sex — having more than once headed her own Troops in Action —— On the death of her husband she succeeded to his Principality, yielding about 90,000 £ per annum. and on the introduction of the British Rule in 1803, she managed with much address to retain her possessions as an Independant Ruler — Her conduct in the internal management of her Estate was highly Commendable — She died at Sirdhanah, the Capital of her Principality in January 1837 at the age of 85 — bequeathing the greater part of her property to an adopted son of the name of Dyce, who assumed also that of Sombre, of some Celebrity in England.

Huzrut Ameer Khoosroo [1] was a man of great and diversified talents. he lived
during the reign of Ghyas-o-deen Bulbun [who reigned from A.D. 1226 to 1236] was born at

1. Respected
2. Literally a Prince.
   Noble.
3. Emperor -

Mominabad in
the Province of
Rohilcund & died
at Dehlie A.D. 13?
He was a disciple of
the Celebrated Saint
Nizam-o-deen - Pag-
grief for whose death
is asserted to have been
the Cause of his own

His Family were originally natives of Bulkh -

Durgah Mukhdoom [2] Subzwaree [3] Saheb.   The individual whose Shrine [1] is here represented
was a native of the Town of Subz in the Province of Kish, and was a person of uncommon talent. When he had acquired
as much learning as his birth place could furnish him with, he proceeded to Shiraz and Bokhara, where he pursued

1. Shrine.
2. Literally a Servant.
4. Title taken from the
   place of birth
1. Emperor.
5. Glory of the Faith.
6. Name of Tribe or
   Family.

his studies in Medicine
and other branches of
Science and Literature
to a perfection which En-
titled him to diplomas
Hence he came to Hin-
doostan during the
reign of Sultan Ala-
odeen Khiljie, who
reigned A.D. 1295 in quest
of Religious Characters
on arrival at Dehlie

became a disciple of Huzrut Sultan ool Mushayek Nizam Odeen Owleea [Page 40] under whom he practised so rigid
a discipline as to induce his Master to nominate him to the succession of the Priesthood held by himself, he did not
however survive to receive the honor having demised about A.D. 1325 two years previous to the death of the Saint -
The Mausoleum & Mosque which are seen in the drawing were erected by his Children.

its shape. The Hooghly Pilots are, in consequence, extraordinarily skilful and also very highly paid – which is not to be wondered at.

The tales of wrecks are endless, and the first time I travelled up the Hooghly to Calcutta, on the SS *City of London*, we could see where the shoal lay because it was clearly marked by the wreck of a river steamer that had run aground on the James and Mary the day before. The steamer had, we were told, only touched the sands: but that was enough, for its prow being held the currents instantly swung it against the main bank, which gripped its keel, and sands and current together made it heel over to one side. In the suddenness of the disaster a great many lives had been lost, and there was no hope of salvage, for the James and Mary does not give back anything it has once caught. The steamer had been a big one, but already all that could be seen of her were the top few feet of her funnels, part of her masts and a very little of her superstructure, through and around which the turgid Hooghly current swirled and chuckled. It was easy to see that soon there would be nothing left except dimpled brown water from bank to bank, and that the steamer would be just another statistic on the long list of ships that have been swallowed by the James and Mary.

Calcutta's "Garden Reach", described by Emily, is where many of the rich East India Company merchants lived in considerable luxury and splendour. Horatia Lawrence, Sir Henry's wife, mentions that while staying in one of these mansions on her arrival in India, and being amazed by the large number of servants, she asked her hostess how many she employed. To which that lady replied: "I'm not sure; but we are very moderate people." The number when actually totted up came to almost thirty – not bad for "moderate people"! We can be sure that Emily's father, who was far from moderate, employed at least three times that number, if not four. However, the popular view taken by the ignorant that all the British in the days of the Raj employed far too many servants (whom they paid far too little), in order to show off or feel important, is in fact, like most popular views, bunk. The reason why householders employed so many is because in that country, even up to Independence (and, I suspect, still), no servant would do any work but his own, so that every household chore had to have a separate person to do it. The *masalchi*, who washed up the dirty dishes, did not put them away – someone else did that. The *bhisti* carried water, but would not water the garden – the *mali* did that. And so on. Such a person as a cook-general had not only never been heard of but could not have been found in all India. It was, like so many other things in that great land, a matter of caste. It was also a very useful thing, for it gave a livelihood to literally millions of people, since each servant, however humble his task, lived in the servants' quarters behind his employer's bungalow, and supported a large family.

When I returned to India in 1963 to do research for *The Far Pavilions*, an old servant of a British officer who had left India when the Raj ended said to me sadly: "Memsahib, in the old days every Sahib, even the youngest ones newly arrived from Belait (England), often employed as many as eight servants. True, the pay was far less than it is now; but then the prices were also much less and so one could support one's family without difficulty. Nowadays, although my pay is more than three or four times greater than it was then, the prices are greater still, and not one but several officers share my services between them, so that very many people are left without work and do not know where to turn to earn bread for their wives and children."

India's princes too – the Maharajahs and Rajahs, the Nawabs and Nizams and Ranas and all the many rulers of independent states – used to employ enormous numbers of servants. But now that their titles have been abolished and they can no longer use the revenues of their one-time kingdoms, they too have had to drastically retrench, and many can afford only one or two servants where once they kept two hundred. One wonders what became of those who had to be dismissed?

*T*here was also the excitement of looking out for alligators on the banks of the river, and for boats coming down from Calcutta with letters for the passengers on board, and finally, as we passed up by Garden Reach, I was enchanted by the Indian-style houses with gardens sloping down to the water, and several things I saw that recalled memories of the days when I was a child in Calcutta.

As we approached the landing-place, we saw groups of ladies and gentlemen awaiting the arrival of their friends on the steamer and I noticed two ladies, one in black, the other in red velvet, who were pointed out to me as Mrs Cameron and Mrs Jackson, coming to meet their newly married sister, Virginia Dalrymple. They were all sisters of Louisa, Henry Vincent Bayley's wife, and of Mrs Toby Prinscep and Lady Somers, daughters of Mr Pattle, of whom in olden days there were many facetious stories in Calcutta, although all *that* is ancient history and of no interest to the present generation. 🌺

Nevertheless, Emily has given a hint as to what those stories were about. "Pattle", spelt with one "t" and not two, is a very well known Hindu name in India, so even though she stops short of repeating the "facetious" gossip one cannot help thinking that she is being a little naughty in referring to it at all!

*U*ncle Benny Colvin came to meet his brother Edward, and gave me a hearty welcome to his house in Kyd Street, where we all drove on leaving the vessel. This was December 8th 1847.

My uncle and aunt received a most kind welcome from his brother Mr Benny Colvin, and an invitation, which included me, to stay with them during the time we spent in Calcutta. I was delighted with everything. It was all so bright and new, and I enjoyed every inch of my life in those days.

When my uncle's servants had got our luggage together, we found a carriage and cart waiting, and were driven to Mr Benny Colvin's house, No. 1 Kyd Street, where I found Mrs Colvin and her children, and received a most affectionate welcome, the beginning of a friendship which lasted through all the years of my life, until she died in 1910 at the age of ninety-three.

The brightness of those first days in India threw a glow over all my Indian experience. The brilliant climate, the beautiful flowers, the gay plumage of the birds, the novelty of all the scenes I witnessed every hour and the lavish hospitality which was then such a marked feature of Indian life, were all new and delightful experiences to me, a simple girl fresh from a very retired home in England.

We stayed in Calcutta a fortnight and I saw a great many friends and connections and many very pretty sights, and the unpacking of all my new and pretty clothes was a source of great amusement. I shall always remember the delight with which I donned my first smart evening dress: a white tarlatan, trimmed with satin ribbon and pink roses. I wore it at a party at Sir Frederick Halliday's, where there was some good orchestral music. I went to several parties in Calcutta, and during the few days that we remained there before resuming our journeyings towards Delhi, was in a constant state of jubilation.

The happiness I experienced on my first arrival threw a halo over all my residence in India, especially over my life in Delhi, and the letters that awaited me in Calcutta from my dear Father were so full of tender love and eager anticipation of our reunion, that they made me intensely happy, and I was most anxious to get to my home as quickly as possible.

But travelling up to the north of India in those days was a very slow process, for the journey had to be made in a small river steamer which crept slowly up the Ganges as far as Allahabad. We ourselves, my uncle and aunt and I, travelled in a large barge attached to the steamer, on the move from daybreak until evening, when we were moored to the bank with strong cords and chains to avoid being carried away by the rush of water down the river at night. When moored we would get out and walk along the bank as long as it was light, and then we used to sit on deck, when some of us would sing. We were a party of some ten or twelve on board; Major Charles Havelock, Captain Read of the Fourteenth Hussars, Mr James Barnes, Mrs Alexander, Mrs Macdonald, Dr Campbell, Mrs McNabb's brother, Major and Mrs Pratt of the Seventh Lancers, and others. The cooking was done on a separate barge that travelled in our wake. 🪰

Emily's return trip up the Ganges from Calcutta to Allahabad must have been a good deal less attractive than her journey down by "budgerow" as a small child. The smoke from the steamer that towed up the barges would have blown back onto them, complete with soot and sparks, and the noise of the paddles as they churned up the Ganges water would have ensured that river turtles, *muggers* (the blunt-nosed, flesh-eating crocodiles of India) and their long-nosed cousins, the fish-eating *garrials*, would have been warned in time and slid back under water long before the boats reached them. Any form of wildlife on shore or on the river would have made itself scarce, and I am grateful when I remember that my own Ganges trip, made in the nineteen-thirties, was downstream, from Garhmuktesar to Narora, in a great, flat-bottomed, wooden-built, open country-boat; oar-powered when necessary, but in general merely allowed to drift down with the stream, instead of having to be pulled against the current.

Emily's voyage took a month, and ours only a fortnight; but like hers it was one of the happiest times of my life. We too passed the sacred city of Benares with its old and lovely jumble of palaces and temples, its long flights of stone steps that come down to the river's edge and are always crowded with people, its burning-ghats and the smoke that rises up from the pyres and makes a haze in the air, so that seen from the river the colours are faintly muted, as though one saw them through a gauze curtain. Less pleasant was the sight of an insufficiently burned corpse that bobbed past our boat on the tide, tugged at from below by fishes and turtles.

*T*his journey by steamer was exactly similar to the journeys now undertaken on the Nile in dahabiehs. The progress was slow against the stream, but the life was most enjoyable and peaceful. It was one continual picnic from morning till night, and for the whole of the month that we were on board we all spent the day on deck under an awning, reading, working or writing letters. We had our meals on deck, and in the evenings when we were moored to the bank, we went on shore for a walk, and then returned again to the deck to spend the evening in pleasant conversation before going to bed.

Oh! dear, I was so happy in those days, all the experiences were so new and delightful, and everyone was so kind to me.

Sometimes there was only a small native village where we anchored for the night, at other times we arrived at a station [*Anglo-Indian term for any town where British officials were stationed* – MMK] and then the residents used to ride or drive down at once to welcome the newcomers on board the steamer, and to offer them all the hospitality in their power. There were more civil stations than military ones on the river then, and we saw some very pretty places, and made some pleasant acquaintances on the way up the river, for in those days the arrival of a party from England caused a great buzz of excitement at every station through which it passed, and many people would pay calls on the strangers passing through. We saw many friends at Patna, and also at Benares where we admired the Hindoo buildings and temples, as well as the ghats, or bathing places, which were crowded with hundreds of people. And then at last we reached Allahabad.

Allahabad (the "City of Allah") where Emily's river journey ended, is known to Hindus as "Prayag" – the "Place of Sacrifice". And to them it is one of the most sacred places in India, for it is here, below a triangular sandspit called the "Sangam", or meeting-place, that the Jumna River joins and becomes one with the Ganges. Legend says that those, and only those, who can truly claim to be sinless can see a line of ripples that marks the place where a third and unseen river rises up out of the earth. When Mahatma Gandhi was murdered in New Delhi, his body was cremated there on the banks of the Jumna. But his ashes were brought to Allahabad to be scattered on the sacred waters – as, later, were the ashes of his friend and disciple, Jawaharlal Nehru.

Those who bathe from the point of the Sangam acquire great merit, and once in every twelve years the Kumbah Mela, the Pilgrims' Fair, is held at Allahabad. At such times countless pilgrims and holy men flock there to pray and bathe themselves in the river; and also to make holiday, for although it is a holy occasion it is also a fair, and for the few weeks in January and February that it lasts, the Sangam and every available scrap of river bank or vacant land is taken over by pilgrims and fakirs of every persuasion. It becomes a vast, roaring town of tents and temporary shelters, while the river itself can barely be seen because of the enormous numbers of the devout who are bathing in it.

*T*he journey had been a most picturesque one, made more so by the different kinds of Indian shipping passing up or down – no English vessels of any kind came up the river so far as this. At Allahabad we found the ghats, the steps up from the river, crowded with friends bringing palanquins, doolies, and all sorts of carrying chairs, to convey us to the spot where the carriages awaited us, and we were taken to a friend's house where we stayed three days, until our luggage was brought up from the steamer.

The stone steps or ghats which led up from the river to the top of the bank were very numerous, although there were not as many as at Benares, where hundreds of Ghats were provided for the benefit of the pilgrims to the town, which is sacred to the Hindoo.

Having consigned our luggage to one of the transit companies to be sent to Delhi, we departed from Allahabad in very rough carriages, drawn by still rougher horses. There was one horse to each carriage, and we each had a carriage with a small amount of luggage on the top, but the animals were generally unbroken and could not be said to be driven by the coachman, for they simply went where they liked and how they liked. Very often one would not start at all for many minutes after everything was ready. The coachman would smack it with his whip, the syce, or groom, would tug at its fore legs with a rope, all to no purpose. Then the syce would collect some straw, put a heap under the animal's body, set it on fire, and then when it became too hot to be pleasant to the horse, it would suddenly dash forward, and gallop at a tremendous rate for the five or six miles that intervened before the next posting-stage.

I described a journey by "dâk-ghari", as these horse-drawn vehicles were called, in *Shadow of the Moon*, and Emily's description of hers tallies with the many other accounts of such journeys that I came across when I was engaged in doing research for that novel. It provides confirmation – if any were needed – that this must have been yet another incredibly uncomfortable way of travelling, for there were no made roads as we understand them, and certainly no rubber tyres on the wheels, while the horses used were untrained and evil-tempered, probably underfed and certainly grossly overworked. Emily and her party were lucky not to meet with the same kind of accident that they suffered in Egypt.

*S*ometimes there were amusing and very awkward experiences. On one occasion, when the horse attached to Uncle Edward's carriage had behaved in this obstinate manner, he had just got out to assist in making the animal start when it suddenly bolted off before he could get into the carriage again, and he was only able to clamber on to the foot-board at the back and stand up there for the whole of that stage; which under a boiling sun was not an agreeable way of travelling. How we laughed and joked during the whole of that journey!

Fortunately, the road called the Grand Trunk Road, which connected Allahabad with Delhi, was perfectly straight and level the whole way, beautifully constructed, so that there was not much danger of accident, even with these obstreperous horses. The distance was four hundred and fifty miles, and it took us a week to accomplish it. The rest-houses, or dâk bungalows, where we had to halt for meals, were square-built thatched erections at the side of the road, with a verandah all round the house. They contained four rooms with a bath-room attached to each room, and the furniture consisted of one table in the centre of the room, one bed (but no bedding) and two or three chairs.

In those days you always carried your bedding with you, as well as a brass basin called a chillumchee, for your ablutions. As soon as you got out of your vehicle, the servant attached to the dâk bungalow came and enquired what you would have to eat, but since all that there was available in those days were fowls, the menu consisted entirely of chicken – roast chicken, boiled chicken, grilled chicken, curried chicken or chicken cutlets. But I must say that those meals, simple as they were, were much relished, and very often they were well cooked and arrived in an astonishingly short time, piping hot.

There was no fresh bread to be had, but the chuppaties made of coarse flour like oatmeal, and deliciously hot, were an excellent substitute. The cook could also make good omelettes, far better than many served at private tables. Fresh goat's milk could also be had, and as travellers always carried their own tea, it was quite possible to get a hearty and satisfactory meal.

Emily's description of a dâk bungalow might have been written at any time between her own day and the one on which the Raj ended in 1947, the only difference being that in most places, though not all, thatch had given place to flat roofs of stone, brick or *muttee* (mud). One still had to provide one's own bedding (although not the "chillumchee", that was provided), and the menu remained identical – chicken in one form or another, eggs, and excellent chuppatis. The *Khansamah* still enquired what the *Huzoor* would like to eat for luncheon (or dinner, as the case might be). But when it came down to brass tacks there turned out to be nothing available but *murgi* – chicken – and all too often travellers would see their luckless dinner being pursued around the compound, cackling with alarm, and hear its frenzied screeching as it was finally captured and decapitated. Chicken served at a dâk bungalow was, in consequence, invariably tough; and no wonder. And if one spent a night there, one's sleep was bound to be disturbed by the howling of jackal packs and the incessant barking of pariah dogs.

*T*ravellers generally made a halt of from two to four hours at these rest-houses, and as we were anxious to push on to Delhi, we never stopped longer than was actually necessary.

The nights were generally spent travelling in these carriages, and then the progress made was not very rapid, for if the occupants of the vehicle went to sleep, the coachman, and often the horse, took the opportunity of doing the same by the side of the road, for some hours during each night.

In those days there was no idea of danger anywhere, and we travelled quite unprotected, little thinking that less than ten years later, that very road would be the scene of such awful tragedies as were enacted in 1857.

When we arrived at Allyghur, I was made intensely happy at receiving a letter from my Father by the hands of one of his own servants. He had sent two of his mounted orderlies to escort us to Delhi, and also three palanquins for my uncle and aunt and myself. The one he sent for me had been made expressly for my Mother, and was now to be my property for all my future journeyings.

We had to give up our horse carriages at this point, because the road to Delhi was not metalled, and I was delighted with my first experience of this new style of travelling. The palanquins were made comfortable with good bedding inside, and doors made to slide, so that they could be shut or opened at pleasure. They were carried by four men, with four more running alongside to change with the others when they were tired, and a torch-bearer with a flaming torch accompanied each palanquin, to run alongside and throw enough light for the bearers to pick their way at night. There was also a man called a banghy-wallah, who carried two tin boxes slung to either end of a long bamboo, which he carried across his shoulder. Everyone in India in those days packed their luggage into these tin pitarahs, as they were the most convenient form of box for the men to carry.

If Emily's memory has not misled her – although I suspect it has – that "*bungy-wallah*" must have been wrongly spelt, since a "*bangi*" is a sweeper – a disposer of night-soil and a man of the lowest caste ("*wallah*" is a slang word meaning "fellow"). It is most unlikely that such a man would have been chosen to carry any personal luggage. Unless Emily is primly disclosing the fact that the very necessary items carried in those tin boxes were portable latrines? That seems far more likely!

One mounted orderly rode alongside my palanquin, while the other was occupied in keeping the three palanquins together, and in looking after the banghy-wallahs. I felt now that I was really getting home, and should see my Father in the course of a few hours, and I was really in an ecstasy of happiness.

It was at Allyghur that we said good-bye to our friend and *"companion de voyage"* Mrs Macdonald, for her husband, Captain Harcourt Macdonald, had come to meet her there, and they started off in quite a different direction. But she remained a kind friend to me throughout her life, and was afterwards my daughter Mary's godmother.

Now the last stage of our journey to Delhi had really begun, and I could not sleep because I was so excited at the thought of seeing Daddy before dawn. At about one o'clock in the morning I looked out of my palanquin, and saw in the glorious moonlight the minarets of the Juma Musjid, the great Mohammedan mosque that is one of the chief beauties of Delhi and of Northern India. As we got nearer I could see the wonderful red walls that surround the city, and I felt I was really getting home, and was wild with excitement. Old servants of my Father's were waiting for me on the road, to give me a welcome.

It was the most marvellous moonlight I have ever seen, and as we crossed the river, the view in both directions with this magnificent city lying before us, was quite wonderful, so many exquisite minarets towering up into the sky belonging to the Mohammedan temples.

At that time, as in the days of my own childhood, the approach to Delhi from the far side of the river was all open country, strewn with ruins and dotted with kikar-trees and clumps of pampas grass. The city itself, with its crenellated walls, its palaces, domes and towers, the soaring minarets and the wide, shimmering ribbon of the Jumna and its white sandbanks curving past it, was always an entrancing sight, and must have been more so in those days. But the bridge of boats that Emily and her party crossed in their palanquins was the same bridge over which, only ten years later, the insurgent troopers of the Third Cavalry, galloping in from Meerut where the Mutiny had broken out on the previous day, rode to bring the dire news to Delhi and urge the King and his subjects to follow their example and massacre the British.

*T*he city was surrounded for many miles by a very high and beautiful red stone wall, but as we went through in the middle of the night, everything was hushed and quiet as we passed these beautiful buildings. We had to cross the whole city of Delhi to reach the gate nearest my Father's house, and as we came nearer and nearer to my home, we were met by knots of the servants come to meet me and bid me welcome. They trotted along beside my palanquin, and at last we reached the Cashmere Gate, which recalled memories of my early childhood, and turned into the road leading to my Father's house.

It was all like magic. Everything so brilliant at two o'clock in the morning, the dazzling moon-light, the deep red of the walls, and the buildings in the city all hushed in perfect quietness and peace as we went through the streets. I was coming home, and as we passed through the orange grove below the house and I saw the great pillars of the verandah above me, my memory recalled the night when I had left that same home with my Mother and little sister in 1835, when I was just over five years of age. I remembered the steps on which I had said good-bye to Father before getting into our palanquins – and here I was back again in the home I had yearned to see all those years.

Soon we were under the great portico and our palanquins were put down in the verandah just before the door of the library, and I rushed in to meet my Father, who received me with the most tender loving affection in my Mother's sitting-room, and there both he and I cried with joy at being together again – but without her!

Our meeting was at 2am on January 20th 1848 – and here I am, dictating this to my darling Mary, on the fifty-fourth anniversary of that day. The rush of memories is quite overwhelming, for all these scenes are as vivid as if they had happened yesterday.

Father was so happy, too, to see my dear aunt and uncle again, and we all sat and had tea together in my Mother's sitting-room.

Our old khansamah, Kajoo by name, brought in the tea and cakes, and I remembered him perfectly from the days of my childhood, and also the old Abdar (wine-bearer).

In about an hour my Father said I had better go to bed, and took me into the next room which was my bedroom, and there I beheld a picture which I had remembered as being in the bow room when I was a child at Delhi. My Father was astonished and delighted to find I had such a good memory. It was that engraving of Sir Joshua Reynolds' well known picture of two children, dark and fair.

These two rooms were allotted to me during the remainder of my life at Delhi, and my Father had collected in them all the pictures and engravings he thought would please me best, besides pretty ebony furniture, clocks, etc. Also many things belonging to my Mother in the shape of workboxes, writing desks and books, all of which he gave over to me.

When I woke the next morning I could scarcely believe that I really was at last at Delhi, and I was in such a flurry of happiness that I had scarcely patience to dress before rushing out to see my Father.

Just as I awoke, I heard a voice calling in the verandah, *"Gurum panee lao"* ("bring hot water"), and what was my surprise to find it proceeding from a large bird in a cage outside my window, a beautiful glossy black minah with a yellow beak, a Nepaulese bird. [*Also common throughout India, except Northern Kashmir, so why Emily calls it a "Nepaulese bird" I do not know. Perhaps this particular one came from there? But it could just as easily have come from Delhi.* MMK] It could speak many Hindoostanee phrases so perfectly as to mislead one into thinking it was some servant speaking, and had learned to copy the inflections of my Father's voice so well that when it called *"Haziri lao"* ("bring breakfast") I often hurried out, thinking it was my Father ordering breakfast to be served.

A large bath-room adjoined my bedroom, and in fact my Father had provided every possible comfort and luxury in order to make my home perfect for me.

Just as I finished dressing, I heard him calling out to me, "Emmie, Emmie!" In another moment I was by his side in the verandah, and he took me into the oratory, a room opening out of his dressing-room, in which he kept all his theological library and sacred pictures, and where we had prayers every morning. This was indeed a sacred place to us both, and my memory often recalls the blessed hours I have spent there with him.

I think I ought to describe my Father as he appeared to me then. He was not a tall man, I should think about 5ft 8in, but well made, with beautifully small hands and feet. His hair was grey, and he was bald on the top of his head, and his eyes were blue. He had a straight nose, a well formed mouth which very often had a whimsical expression on it, but as he retained a good many smallpox marks from his boyhood he could not be said to be a handsome man. He was very sprightly in all his movements, and had a very pleasant voice: a perfect gentleman, every inch of him. He was also the pink of tidiness in his appearance and habits, and his clothes were always extremely well made by a first-class London tailor, Pulford, in St James Street, and sent out regularly every year. His shoes and gloves were of the very best, and everything about him showed perfect taste. He wore only one ring, a signet ring on his little finger.

My Father's bedroom and dressing-room adjoined my sitting-room. He always got up at five o'clock every morning, and having put on his dressing-gown he would go into the verandah and have his "*chota haziri*" (small breakfast). He used to take a walk up and down the verandah, and his different servants came at that time to receive their orders for the day. At seven o'clock he would go down to the swimming bath which he had built just below that corner of the verandah, and then, having dressed and had prayers in the oratory, he was ready for breakfast at eight o'clock punctually.

Everything was ordered with the greatest punctuality, and all the household arrangements moved as by clock work. After he had had his breakfast, his hookah was brought in and placed behind his chair. It stood on an embroidered carpet worked for him by some lady friends, and was a beautiful erection in itself. The stand was of solid silver about eighteen inches in diameter at the bottom, while the cup for the sweet-smelling tobacco mixture which he smoked was of beautifully embossed silver, with silver chains hanging from it. The snake-like pipe was about six to eight feet long, and the mouth-piece at the end of it was exquisitely wrought in silver. By his side on the table a soup plate of water was always placed, and he took the mouth-piece and passed it through the water for fear there should be any animal in it before attaching it to the pipe. He smoked for about half an hour, and the gurgle of the hookah still rings in my ears, a most musical sound.

After he had finished his smoke, he generally went to his study to write letters until the carriage was announced. This always appeared punctually at ten o'clock under the portico, and he passed through a row of servants on his way to it – one holding his hat, another his gloves, another his handkerchief, another his gold-headed cane, and another his despatch box. These having been put into the carriage, his Jemadar mounted beside the coachman and he drove away, with two syces standing up behind. He kept two pairs of horses, one pair of chestnuts, and one of bays; the former generally used in the daytime and the latter for the evening.

Oh, the wild happiness of those first days! Every experience was so new and so delightful, and there was so much to see in every room in the house, such beautiful pictures, furniture, books and ornaments, that my whole day was taken up in admiration and amazement over all that was so new to me. The rooms were so large, so lofty, and there were so many of them, all on one floor, and all twenty-four feet in height. Study, library and Napoleon Gallery in one line faced the north portico; then the drawing-room and banqueting-room behind them facing east and west; then the day-room and small drawing-room, the dining-room and serving-room. These opened into the oratory and lobby, off which opened the large spare bedroom and dressing-room and my Father's dressing-room. Then facing the south verandah, my Father's bed-room, my Mother's sitting-room and my bedroom.

Round all four sides of the house was a splendid verandah, twenty to thirty feet wide and very lofty, the roof supported by magnificent stone pillars. It was a glorious house, and everything in it was really beautiful, although some of the furniture struck newcomers to India as heavy and old-fashioned. But then it was hardly possible to avoid this, as of course it was the style of those days: solid mahogany, rosewood and marble. Many of the tables were entirely of marble, tops, pedestals and all, and very beautiful they were. The books in the different rooms were all beautifully bound, those in my Father's study being bound in Russian leather. He got out a box of books from England twice a year, and during his forty years of residence in India he had gathered together a very valuable library of five-and-twenty thousand volumes, all of which were to be destroyed in the Mutiny of 1857.

He had a great love for engravings, and the walls of the house in 🐎

every room were covered with engravings of well known persons and of events of historical interest, which today would fetch enormous prices. But the only relics of all this collection are the engraving of Napoleon and the Wilkie pictures I possess; and even these have been injured by the climate of India. In every room there were handsome silver inkstands and paper-knives and clocks, and my dear old Dad could not bear to have these removed from their proper places.

The room called the "Napoleon Gallery", which was in the northeast corner of the house, was entirely devoted to the memory of Napoleon Buonaparte, of whom as I have said my Father was a devoted admirer. Its bookcases were filled with all the best and most interesting works relating to his life and career, and the walls were covered with fine engravings: portraits of the great hero, of his generals, and of all the events of his life. In one corner of the room on a marble pedestal stood Canova's marble bust of Napoleon, a beautiful work of art of which I now possess only the broken pieces, which I gathered out of the ruins of the house at Delhi two years after the Mutiny.

The centre and side tables in the Napoleon Gallery were covered with beautiful bronzes and statuettes, all connected with the history of the Emperor. One especially fine bronze, three feet long, depicted the fight of the Bridge of Lodi, but this, like everything else, was either destroyed or carried off on the day the house was looted in the middle of May 1857. On the centre table, under a glass case, there was a beautiful marble stand with an exquisite silver statuette of Napoleon, and below the figure were hung the Napoleon gem, which I possess, the Cross of the Legion of Honour, and his diamond ring with the initial on it, which my Father purchased after the death of Mr Fraser, to whom they had all been sent by Napoleon's desire, in acknowledgement of the courteous and generous gift which he despatched to St Helena for the use of the Emperor, but which was lost at sea, and therefore never reached the exiled hero.

The cross and ring were left to my eldest brother and were destroyed on the day the house was looted, as my brother was still resident at Delhi. But fortunately I had taken the Napoleon gem with me to England in 1854.

It was in this gallery that my Father used to sit every afternoon after his midday meal to refresh himself by reading before going

down to the billiard room in the tajkhanah underground. This daily
game at billiards was not only a great amusement to him, but gave
him the exercise he required, and when he had finished his game he
always went directly to the chibootra, or terrace, overhanging the
river, where three or four chairs were placed, and where he sat for a
couple of hours till it was time to dress for dinner in the evening. It
was the custom for his friends to come at this time to see and chat
with him as he sat on the chibootra.

He returned from the office every day at half-past two, having
established the custom of dinner at three o'clock, as he found that
was conducive to his health. And in the evening he made only a very
light meal, for it was his invariable custom to leave the dining-room
at eight o'clock in order to go to bed early. It used to be a great
source of amusement to Aunt Mary and me to watch his proceedings as soon as the "retiring gun" fired and the clock struck eight.
He immediately got up from the chair where he was smoking his
hookah, said good-night to everyone at the table, undid his
neck-cloth and threw it on the ground while he was walking to the
door, unfastened his waistcoat buttons and then turned and gave a
wave of his hand as he disappeared behind the curtain into his
dressing-room. Sometimes if I was alone with him he actually took
off his coat and flung it aside before he got to the door. But
whenever we had guests in the house, or at his periodical parties, of
course he conformed to the usual customs, and did not retire until
after his guests had left. Dear, dear Daddy! he was so full of fun, so
witty, constantly making good puns. And having a great fund of
anecdote he was always capital company.

He was an excessively fastidious man, and very particular as to
the habits of ladies. He could not bear to see them eat cheese, and as
for eating mangoes and oranges he thought ladies ought to indulge
in them only in the privacy of the bath-room. Many a time have I,
with Colonel Richard Lawrence, taken a basket of oranges to the
top of the Kutub Minar, two hundred and eighty-three feet high, to
indulge in a feast in that seclusion, taking care to bring down all the
peel, etc., with us, as nothing disorderly was allowed within the
precincts of those beautiful ruins and buildings. ✣

I do not understand why Emily's father objected to seeing women eating
cheese. Did he perhaps connect cheese with ploughmen? (In England, to

Continued on page 141

Umbaree Tangah or covered Conveyance used by the Rajah of Bhurtpoor.

Nalkee or Covered Sedan for the Queen. or Ladies of First Rank —

130

The Fukhrool-Musajid was built by Kuneez i Fatima
widow of Shoojaat Khan about A.D. 1729, to the memory of her
husband who was one of the confidential followers of Nizam'ool
Moolk, Minister of Mohummud Shah. Page 12. It adjoins the
Estate and is nearly opposite to the Church erected by the late Colonel Skinner C.B.
and has been of late years repaired at no inconsiderable expense by that distinguished Officer- for   the conveni-
ence of his   followers Military and   Menial. —

1. Pride of Mosques   4. Regulator of the State.
2. Slave.   5. Praised.
3. Name of the daughter   6. Emperor.
   of the Prophet.

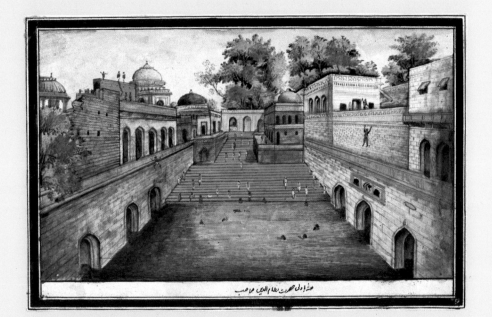

A celebrated Boulee, or deep Reservoir adjoining to the Shrine
of the Saint Nizamoodeen. Page 40. It is much resorted to
by Travellers, to witness the feats of Divers who are located at
the place, and Jump from a considerable height into the
Reservoir.—

Feroze[1] Shah's[2] Laut[3] is situated in the immediate Environs of the City on the High Road from the Dehlie Gate towards Muttra — The Building on which the Laut[3] now stands was constructed by the Emperor Feroze[1] Shah[2] as a Shekargah or Hunting place — He reigned at Dehlie between the years AD. 1351 and 1388 in the last of which he died at the Age of 90 — but the Pillar must have been erected as a Hindoo Monument, at a much earlier period, for one of the Inscriptions records a date of 1220 of the Hindoo Æra, corresponding with AD. 1164. or 29 years before the Conquest of Dehlie by Shahabodeen[4] Ghoree[5] — The height of the Pillar now visible, above the building is about 37 feet, and its circumferences where it joins the Terrace is 10 feet 4 inches; it is composed of a Single Stone, and tradition asserts that only 1/3 is visible, the remaining 2/3ds being buried in the Earth — The Structure originally consisted of three Stories, and used, according to Current Opinion, partly, as a Menagerie and partly as an aviary —

The Emperor's reign of 38 years, though not brilliant in other respects was distinguished for the Enlightened spirit of his Regulations and the extent and utility of his Public Works — amongst the latter, and the greatest of all is the Canal from the Jumna to the district of Hansie and Hissar and still called by his name —

1 Propitious

2 King

3 Pillar - Club —

4 Strength of the Faith

5 Name of a particular Family or

   Dynasty.

the second View represents a Portion of the old Palace built by the same Emperor, but now
fast falling into decay. On my first arrival arrival at Dehly in 1813, and indeed for many

خستہ کو تکلیف نو دن ، ما دن .

Years subsequent, the Hall of Audience here represented was in perfect condition. The Roof
has of late fallen in with part of the front Wall, and a Portion of the Room in which the Emperor Alumgeer the 2d was murdered, and the Door way nearest to the River (as shewn in the draw
ing) still exists, through which the life-less body of the Emperor was Cast out upon the sand, where
it lay for several Days uninterred and almost unnoticed.

منظر کو تکلیف نو دن ، ہر جانب دریا .

In the back ground are seen the Minarets of the Zeenut ool Musajid (Vide page 33) and the
Bridge of Boats constructed by the Local Authorities over the River Jumna.
The Emperor Ahmed Shah having been deposed and blinded in July A.D: 1754, by Ghazeeodeen
his Commander in Chief, one of the Princes of the Blood Royal, a son of the former Emperor Jehandar

Shah

Shah was fixed on as the Successor and proclaimed by the Title of Alumgeer II.

Soon after this Revolution, the Minister Sufdur Jung (Vide page 24) died and Ghazee-roodeen took the Office of Minister to himself. A longer period of Tranquillity now elapsed than might have been expected from the restless ambition of this new Wuzeer: but his internal Government was as arbitrary as ever: so that at length he provoked a numerous body of troops to Mutiny, who seized his person and dragged him through the Streets in a most de-grading Manner. Having however been rescued through the interposition of his Officers he instantly ordered a Massacre of the whole body, giving up their Tents, Houses and Property to Plunder, so as not to leave a Vestige remaining of the Corps. In this unfortunate Reign, Dehly was subjected to a third Invasion from Ahmed Shah, the Dooranee, or Afghan Monarch, and nearly all the Horrors of Nadir Shah's Invasion (Vide page 17) were repeated. On the departure of the Afghan King, having been entreated by the Emperor not to leave him at the Mercy of his Minister, Ghazeeroodeen, he appointed Nujeeb'ood Dowläh his Commander in Chief, in hopes that he would act as a Counterpoise to to the all powerful Minister. this was in A.D. 1757. but on Ahmed Shah's subsequent advance into India in 1759, the Minister being Apprehensive of the Emperor's Connexion with the Afghan Monarch and Nujeeb'ood Dowlah, induced his Master under the Plea of Visiting a religious Devotee of great Sanctity to repair to the old Palace of Feroze Shah and there caused him to be assassinated by persons concealed for the Purpose. The body was thrown out upon the Sands below as before stated, but subsequently interred at Hoomaeoun's Tomb (Vide Page 9) ——————

1 Praise worthy   4 The Ruler of the World
2 'King   5 The Conqueror of the World
3 the Hero of the Faith. 6 The Exalted of the State

——————————————

Shére Sháh's (or more commonly called the Old) Fort is situated about 4 miles to the S: East and between the City of Dehly and the Tomb of the Emperor Hoomaioon (Vide Page   ). Its construction is attributed to Shére Khän who was destined to act so great a part in the eventful History of the above named Emperor.

Ibraheem Khän, the Grand father was a native of Afghanistan and both he and his son Hússun were married into noble Families of their own Nation.

The latter held a Jageer at Sasseram in the lower Provinces of India for the Maintenance of 500 Horse. He had two Sons, the eldest Shére Khan, and when of an age to act for himself left his Father and entered as a private Soldier in the Service of the Governor of Juanpoor. Here he devoted himself to study. made himself familiar with History and Poetry and acquired a general Knowledge of other branches of Information. He afterwards proceeded to Dehly and took service with Sooltan Secundur

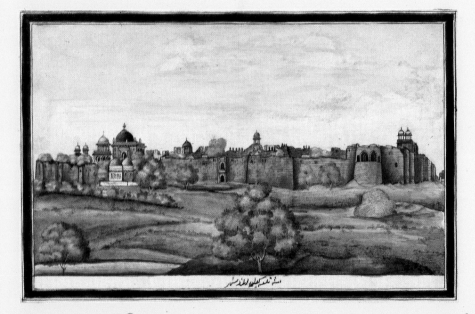

Shére King, who died in A.D. 1517. and remained there until the death of his Father when he returned to the family Jageer. Having raised himself by his own daring to High Military Rank. He acted a conspicuous part in the tumults that devastated not only the Province of Behar in which he was born, but also of Juanpoor in which he first enlisted as a Soldier. Siding at first with Mohummed Shah Lãdani (A.D. 1526) against the Emperor Baber. then with the Governor of Juanpoor on the part of the Emperor (A.D. 1527) against his late Master - joining the Emperor in 1528 and obtaining from him a Command in Behar. and again in the next Year returning to the Standard of Mohummed Shah, and on the dispersion of the Army of the latter in the same Year renewing his submission to the Emperor.

The Emperor Baber died in A.D. 1530, at Agra and was succeeded by his Son Hooma -ioon. during the early part of Hoomaioon's reign, Shérekhan made himself Master of the Provinces

ƒ

of Behar, obtained possession of the Fort of Chunar and of the still more important Fortress of Rohtas. The latter taken by Treachery, having persuaded the Rajah or chief to give an Asylum to his Family, he introduced armed Soldiers in the covered litters which were supposed to conceal the Females.

In A.D. 1535/6, the Emperor Hoomaioon found it necessary to march in person to check if not subdue this ambitious Soldier. Success in part followed the Royal Army, until the Spirit of the Soldiers sunk under the moist and sultry climate of Bengal and their numbers were thinned by the sickly season that followed the periodical and heavy Rains. No sooner were the Roads suited for travelling, than the troops deserted in numbers. The Emperor was compelled to retreat, but was intercepted by Shere Shah, and after a delay of several Months, the Emperor's camp was completely surprised and dispersed. Hoomaioon had not a Moment for deliberation, but plunged at once on Horseback into the Ganges. Before he could reach the opposite Bank, the Horse was exhausted and sunk into the Stream - and the Emperor must himself have met with the same fate if he had not been saved by a Water Carrier who was crossing the River with the aid of the Skin used to hold Water and which inflated as a Bladder, supported the King's weight as well as his own.

Hoomaioon fled to Dehly A.D. 1539, but in the next year again took the Field against Shere Shah. A general Action ensued in which he was entirely and finally defeated. His Army driven into the Ganges. Himself in imminent Danger - His Horse wounded and he must have been either killed or taken, if he had not fortunately found an Elephant on which he mounted, and compelled one of those whom he found with the Animal to take to the Stream. The opposite Bank was too steep for the Elephant to ascend and Hoomaioon must still have perished had not two Soldiers who happened to have gained that part of the Shore, tied their Turbans together and by throwing one end to the Emperor, enabled him to make good his landing.

Hoomaioon fled to Lahore and eventually to Persia.

The ultimate success of the Seeroor family has occasioned Shere Shah to be considered as an Usurper; yet as he was born in India, and expelled a foreign family who had only been fourteen years in possession, his claim was in reality more conformable to Justice than those of most Founders of Dynasties in that Country. Having taken Possession of all Hoomaioons Dominions, Shere Shah, for he now assumed the Title of King, next proceeded to conquer Malwa. From thence he invaded Marwar - took Chittour and laid Siege to Kalingur. Here as he was superintending the Batteries, he was involved in the Explosion of a Magazine, which had been struck by the

Enemies

Enemy's Shot, and was so scorched that he expired a few Hours afterwards.

In the midst of his Agonies he continued to direct the operations of the Siege and when intelligence was brought to him that the place was taken, he exclaimed "Thanks be to Almighty God", and never spake again.

Shere Shah was a Prince of consummate Prudence and Ability - His Ambition was too strong for his Principles, but his measures were as Benevolent in their Intentions as were those in Conduct.

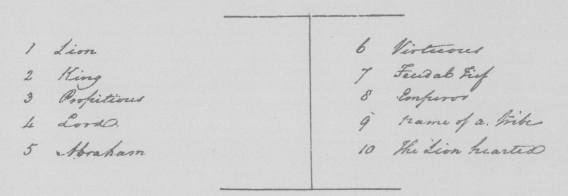

1 Lion
2 King
3 Propitious
4 Lord
5 Abraham
6 Virtuous
7 Feudal Fief
8 Emperor
9 Name of a Tribe
10 The Lion hearted

The Mosque attached to the Old Fort, built at the same time and by the same Individual

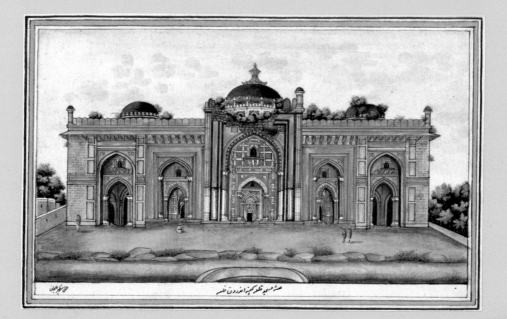

The Musjid Killan[1][2] or large Mosque, but from its sombre Appearance denominated by Europeans the Kalee or Black Mosque was constructed in the Reign of the Emperor Feroze Shah,[3][4] who flourished between 1351 and 1388, by one Khan-è Juhan,[5] whose Tomb is within the Building

Although included within the present City built by the Emperor Shah Juhan[6] and called after him Shah Juhanabad[7] this Mosque must have existed certainly for two Centuries before

It is in the rudest Style of Patan Architecture, with a succession of 34 Small domes on the Top and a steep ascent of 32 Steps - It is now completely surrounded by Houses and indeed is situated in the Most Populous part of the City.   For many Years, Previous to 1822 it had been occupied by a Colony of Silk Manufacturers, who were somewhat indignant at their Ejection from a Commodious habitation. merely to gratify the Taste of their European Rulers, for improvements and it so happened that in 1823/24 when undergoing Repairs, by some untoward Chance, the Black Mosque was White washed and it was estimated that the Sum of Rs 3000. would be required to restore it to its former antiquated Appearance.

1 Mosque, Mahomedan Place of Worship	5 Lord of the World
2 Great. applicable also to Person	6 King of the World
3 Prohibitions	7 City or abode of Shah Juhan the King of the World
4 King	8 Particular Race and Dynasty

نقشه مسجد کلان عرف کالی

A Tangah or conveyance without Cover — also used by the Rajah of Bhurtpoor.

A Ruth or Covered Vehicle for Ladies of Rank.

this day, a "ploughman's lunch", which can be had at almost any pub in the land, consists of bread and butter with cheese and pickles.) Or did he see cheese as something one ate with port after the ladies had retired? As for the mangoes, my own father, too, was of the opinion that the only really suitable place to eat one was while sitting in the bath, and no one can deny that they are one of the messiest fruits to eat, even though I, personally, would rank a ripe "dessert" mango – one of the Alphonse variety – among the most delicious of fruits. Unfortunately, the "com-mon-or-garden" mango does not come into this category, for apart from having rather hairy flesh it is apt to taste very faintly of turpentine – a flavour that vanishes when it is cooked, which is why the ordinary mango is seldom eaten raw in India except by the poor, but is used to make chutneys, pickles or mango-fool.

Tourists returning from the East who speak rudely of mangoes have been fobbed off with this variety and never tasted an Alphonse one; and almost certainly they have smeared their clothes, hands and faces with thick yellow juice!

All the same, I feel that Emily's "dear old Daddy" was being a bit over-pernickety to bracket mangoes with oranges, and I applaud both her devotion to them and her energy in climbing to the top of the Kutub Minar in order to eat the forbidden fruit in seclusion. I cannot remember how many steps there are to the top, only that there are a great many, and that the last time I climbed the Minar I could barely crawl up the last twenty or so. On the other hand, I clearly remember my sister and myself running up and down again twice in one day when we were children, so the seventeen-year-old Emily probably took it in her stride, and the one to feel sorry for is poor Colonel Lawrence.

When I first read Emily's diary, my instant reaction was: "Why out to the Kutub, for heaven's sake? It's *miles* from Metcalfe House!" But then I remembered that her father had bought two tombs that stand in a corner of the Kutub grounds, and turned one of them into a sort of week-end retreat which he named Dil-Koosha, but which was always known locally as "Metcalfe's house". So in fact Emily and Richard Lawrence would have had only to walk across the garden with their basket of oranges to reach the entrance to the Minar.

*M*y father was very anxious to introduce me at once to the many residents of Delhi with whom he was on very friendly terms, and who were all anxious to see his daughter. He himself took me to pay some of these visits, while my Aunt Mary chaperoned me to others.

One of the first visits I made with my Father was to Mrs John Gubbins, who lived in a delightful house near the church. She had been a Miss Egerton of the well known Cheshire family, was tall, fair and good-looking, and an angel in character and disposition. Mr Gubbins was a short, dark man, and held the post of Judge at Delhi. He was a man of very fiery temper, but a true-hearted friend – the friendship begun at Delhi lasted throughout life. Mrs Fred Gubbins was at that time living with them, and forty years later we two were again thrown a great deal together, when she was living at Ascot with the Duchess of St Albans, who was Mr Gubbins' sister.

Another visit, the same day, was paid to the two Miss Robertsons, who lived with their brother Major Robertson over the principal gateway of the King's Palace, as he was the official assistant to my Father, and represented British authority in the Palace. The Robertsons were all true and kind friends, and fortunately for them they left Delhi before the Mutiny took place, for on May 11th 1857 all English people who occupied those rooms were murdered while at the breakfast table: among them were the Reverend and Miss Jennings, who were dear friends of mine, for Margaret Jennings had been brought up with me at Belstead.

From the palace we went to pay a visit to a worthy missionary and his family, for whom my father had a great esteem: the Reverend David Thompson. [*Was this, perhaps, the Thompson who did those charming little pencil sketches that appear in Sir Thomas' "Delhie Book"?* MMK] Due notice had been given them of this intended visit, and when we arrived at the door Mr Thompson was waiting to receive us, dressed in evening dress clothes, black hat and white kid gloves.

He and his family were all very dark, having a great deal of native blood in their veins, and this accounted for their utter ignorance of English customs as regards dress. As these visits were all paid in the forenoon, before luncheon, which in those days was the universal custom in India, you may therefore imagine my astonishment on being ushered into the drawing-room to find Mrs Thompson and five daughters waiting to receive me, seated in a row and wearing white gloves and white cotton dresses with low necks and short sleeves, while embroidered Delhi scarves of brilliant colours were

thrown over the necks of some of the ladies. The two sons were, like
their father, in full evening dress with white kid gloves.

They were a most worthy family, and gave me the kindliest
greeting, for they were much attached to my Father, who had
always been a very kind friend to them. This whole family, except
for one daughter, was wiped out on May 11th 1857, being murdered
by the mutineers as they rushed through that part of the city. The
only daughter to survive happened to be at that time at Meerut,
forty-five miles off, where the Mutiny broke out on Sunday May
10th; and she had just time to send a telegram to her father, warning
him that the mutineers were marching from Meerut to Delhi, before
the wire was cut. But the telegram was not delivered until very late
on Sunday night. Before anyone could recover from their astonishment or make arrangements for flight, the mutineers arrived early
on Monday morning, and entered the city by the Palace Gates
which were opened for them.

On our way homewards that day we paid one more call, and that
was on a Mrs Foster, who lived close to the Cashmere Gate. She was
the widow of a celebrated officer, Colonel Foster, who raised and
commanded a distinguished regiment, the Shekawattee battalion, in
the early part of the century. Both Mrs Foster and her sister Mrs
Fuller were enormously stout people, and, being half-castes, were
dark in complexion and spoke English with a very curious accent.
And as both were dressed in white cotton dresses made very like
bed-gowns, they presented a curious spectacle to a newcomer.

They were, however, excellent old ladies, and their sons and
daughters were all connected with the British Army in India. But
both of them unfortunately met their deaths on the day of the
Mutiny at Delhi. I do not know if they were wounded by the
sepoys, but they had been let down from their own house, which
stood close to the city walls, by faithful servants into the dry moat
which lay at the foot of the wall. This was done to facilitate their
escape, but they were too old and too corpulent to climb on to the
level ground, and they are said to have died in the ditch from fits or
sunstroke. ❧

Emily's information is incorrect. I do not know what happened to poor
Mrs Fuller – perhaps she was lucky enough to die quickly at the hands of
the mob? But Lieutenant Edward Vibart of the 54th Native Infantry

records that Mrs Foster was one of a number of women who had taken refuge in a guardhouse (blockhouse?) on the top of the wall near the Kashmir Gate. When the sepoys inside the gate turned on the British officers and started shooting them down, those who could ran up the slope leading to the battlements and began to jump over the wall. Vibart recalls that at this point feminine shrieks from the blockhouse reminded them of the women and, fetching them out, they lowered them over the wall on life-lines made out of the officers' belts hurriedly buckled or knotted together. However, when it came to Mrs Foster's turn, the poor old lady resisted so hysterically that in the end, says Vibart, they "lost all patience and pushed her".

He goes on to describe how, when the mutineers had rushed off to join in the looting of St James's Church and nearby European-owned houses, the men who had jumped into the dry moat helped the women across, and with great difficulty pushed them up the steep bank on the far side, from where they ran for the shelter of the trees and bushes in the Kudsia Bagh. Mrs Foster, who apart from being very fat had been badly bruised by her fall from the top of the wall, was still hysterical (which is not surprising) and since she was unable to help herself, they had no ordinary time pushing, shoving and hauling the bulky dame up the bank. Once there, she had to be carried, but by the time they reached the Kudsia Bagh the panting officers found that it was not possible to tote this moaning and unmanageable load through the bushes and the tangled undergrowth, so they abandoned the attempt and dumped her there. Vibart expresses the opinion that she must have been so badly injured by her fall that the chances were that she would be dead before the mutineers found her, and adds piously: "God rest her soul." General John Nicholson, who took a refreshingly forthright view on the problems posed by women and children in times of military crisis, would have approved.

*M*y next tour of visits was to the families in cantonments, and dear Aunt Mary took me on that occasion, to call first on a Mrs Stuart Menteith, a very pretty woman, with a large family, one of whom had just arrived from England as a grown-up daughter. There was staying in the house a very handsome widow, Mrs Allister Stuart, who afterwards became Mrs Douglas Campbell and was well known to my children at Simla as Mrs "Duggie" Campbell (she had at one time been engaged to Dan Bayley, but his mother forbade the marriage).

Afterwards we paid a visit to Mrs Polwhell, who had been a friend of my Mother's and was always very kind to me. I saw her last at Cheltenham in March 1884.

There were at that time three regiments of native infantry quartered in cantonments, and I was taken to call on the wives of all the officers. Some of them lived in miserable houses, and were evidently in very straitened circumstances, but all gave me a kindly greeting, and I have often wondered since how they could be so cheerful, when their husbands had such a small pittance to live on. But living was then very cheap in India, and as everyone was very simple and kindly life's burdens were much lightened. Really at that time there was no amusement in Delhi, except an annual ball on the Queen's birthday at the Assembly Rooms, and an occasional dinner party at some of the residents' houses.

The numbers of the Regiments were the 4th N.I.; 30th N.I.; 42nd N.I.; and a battery of artillery. The station was commanded by a Colonel Palmer, a portly old gentleman, a "bon-vivant".

When I arrived at Delhi my Father was performing the duties of the chaplain at the church, as his friend Mr Loveday had just died, and it was the custom in India for the Senior Civilian to take this duty during the illness or absence of a regular Chaplain. My Father had had to fill this office many times during his residence in Delhi, and had consequently purchased a number of books of the best sermons to read at the various services. His theological library was divided between us at his death, and I have also a memorandum of all the sermons he preached at church, from the time of my arrival until after my marriage.

The first chaplain appointed after I arrived in Delhi was a Mr Boyle, a wild Irishman, who with his wife was received and treated with the greatest hospitality by my Father for several weeks after their arrival. He was afterwards killed at Sealkot, when there was a rising during the Mutiny. His wife had formerly been a Miss Claxton whom I had seen at Clifton before I left England, but, poor little lady, she had a very rough time of it in India, being very badly off. I lost sight of her when she left India in bad health, but I know she is now dead.

There was one very queer old couple at Delhi, Dr and Mrs Ross, both short and corpulent, broad as they were tall, and very ugly. They were kindly old souls, but he was a shocking bad doctor. At

any rate his medical knowledge was much behind the times, and he
nearly killed me with his violent remedies. When they left Delhi my
Father gave them each fifty pounds with which to buy a magnificent
watch and chain, which they afterwards showed me with great
pride, when I returned to England.

One of their daughters, who came out to India the same year that
I did, was one of my bridesmaids. She afterwards married a Captain
Barwell, and was murdered at Hansi, in the Delhi Division, two
days after Uncle Theo had been staying with her on his flight from
Delhi.

As soon as all the first visits had been paid, my Father took me
out to spend a few days at the Kutub, where he had built another
house, and it was always a refreshment to him to go there when he
could spare a few days from his regular attendance at office.

It was a delightful residence, and a very quaint one, for it was
originally a Mohammedan tomb, surrounded by a big stone dome.
The family to whom it belonged had become impoverished, and had
handed over this tomb as the only available asset to the banker to
whom they owed a large sum of money. He wished to sell it, and so
my Father bought it, but, making no use of the ground floor below
which the tomb lay, built a suite of rooms in the verandah
surrounding the central hall above, which he used as a dining-room.
The building was octagonal in shape and consisted of my Father's
bedroom and library, a drawing-room and my bedroom, a spare
bedroom and dressing-room, a tiny room called an oratory, and
two entrance halls, east and west, which were reached by flights of
steps from the outside.

Strangely enough, the other tomb, built by his mother for Adham Khan,
was also eventually made over, in lieu of cash, as repayment of debts owed
by his descendants to a banker – who in turn sold it to Emily's father. One
presumes that Sir Thomas bought it in order to save it from being pulled
down and the stone used for building material, or else to prevent someone
else from converting it into a house which would destroy the privacy of his
Dil-Koosha. I am told that nowadays guides who take parties of tourists
through the ruins that surround the Kutub Minar will often tell their
gullible charges that this particular tomb is that of our first forefather,
Adam himself (the pronunciation is the same). It makes a nice story, but
the true one is more gory. Moreover, there are two versions of it (and for

all I know, this being India, even more!). I have chosen the one I first heard – the Delhi version.

Adham Khan's mother, Maham Anagah, was one of the Emperor Akbar's fostermothers, the other being the wife of a gentleman called Shams-ud-din Muhammad, who became Governor of the Punjab and was eventually made Prime Minister by the young Akbar, who had hitherto been very much under the thumb of Maham Anagah and her son. Those two, probably scenting a rival, were reluctant to share power, and a day came when Adham Khan, who had clearly become swollen-headed, traded once too often on ranking as the Emperor's fosterbrother. He strolled calmly into a room in the palace where the new Prime Minister was at work, and stabbed him to death.

Akbar, hearing the resulting uproar, ran out of his private apartments, and, when his fosterbrother attempted to seize his hands and sue for pardon, wrenched them away and knocked the murderer down with a well placed blow on the jaw. After which he ordered his guards to take the wretched man up to the topmost terrace of the palace and throw him down into the courtyard below – not once (although once was more than enough) but twice. The battered corpse having duly been carried up and thrown down again, the bodies of both murderer and victim were sent to Delhi (Akbar's court was at that time in Agra), where the latter was buried near the Jam'at Khana Mosque, while Adham Khan's body was taken out to the Kutub to be buried by his mother in a red sandstone tomb of what is known as "middle Pathan design". Maham Anagah is said to have been so overcome with grief that she died of a broken heart only forty days after her son was killed, and was buried beside him, but the stone that once marked her grave has disappeared, although his is still there. One can feel sorry for her, even though she was an ambitious schemer: but not for him. This is no place to tell of his ugly doings, but he was not only a cold-blooded killer who would have made a nineteen-twenties Chicago gangster seem tame by contrast, he was also a thoroughly bad lot who richly deserved his end.

*R*ound the house he laid out a very pleasant garden, and built three or four rooms for the accommodation of gentlemen in the garden. Our house was called the Dil-Koosha (the delight of the heart) and was constantly lent by my Father to bridal parties for their honeymoons. It was a most enjoyable spot in itself, and had also the additional charm of being close to the beautiful Kutub Minar, the great historical tower, and all the wonderful ruins surrounding it. The grounds on which the tower and ruins stood had been laid out, at my Father's suggestion, as a beautiful garden, and the place was kept scrupulously clean and in excellent repair.

To continue the story of our daily life, Aunt Mary and Uncle Edward came out to join us and enjoyed their visit greatly, as they had not seen the house since it was finished. My Father carried out his usual plan of sitting on the chibootra every evening after the heat of the day, and here, below the chibootra, was a building full of pigeons which used to be let loose of an evening and amused us all by their fantastic pranks.

All the waste ground in the neighbourhood of the Kutub was very rocky, and extended for miles without a building of any kind. The ground, owing to its rocky nature, was very barren, so that beyond a few stunted trees there was nothing to relieve the eye; and as my Father's favourite amusement was brick and mortar, he designed and built at some distance off, on high ground, a lighthouse and a small fort – or, rather, a building that looked like a fort, with a castellated wall. These created a diversion from the level monotony of the rocky ground and, as my Father always had a light put in each of the buildings on the nights that we stayed at the Dil-Koosha, we could see the buildings as we sat on the chibootra of an evening, and fifty years afterwards to my amazement, in a picture exhibition in Bond Street, I saw a watercolour drawing of this same little fortress, entitled "The Metcalfe Battery". The clever artist had made a very effective picture of this rough little building, surrounded by rocky ground, a dark mass against a brilliant sunset sky.

My Father had gathered together a very good library here, and also a number of fine engravings and pretty ornaments, so that it was really a very tasteful little abode, and I loved it dearly. It was so well known as a charming residence that when the Mutiny broke out in 1857 the King of Delhi sent out a guard and took possession of the place, with strict orders that nothing was to be touched, but kept strictly guarded, as the King himself intended to come and live there.

To this fact we owe the recovery of some books which were left to Uncle Charlie, the dressing case with silver fittings which was in my Father's bedroom and which was also left to him, and the marble panel with a prayer engraved on it, which used to be in my Father's bedroom, and which I now possess at Ascot. The set of Wilkie's engravings and the portrait of Napoleon, now at the Wilderness, were also preserved in this way, together with the small round mahogany table with grey marble top which came out of the tiny room that my Father called the oratory. This we purchased from the estate after my Father's death and brought home with us to England in 1854.

In fact, all the articles I possess from the old home at Delhi were purchased by us at that time; viz: the big French clock, with the gilt man and horse; the carved ebony stand and flower basket; the two carved ottomans; and the ebony cabinet containing shells. These were the only things that were saved that had belonged to the house at Delhi, and they had been safely housed in England before the Mutiny broke out.

As there was was no church within reach of the Dil-Koosha, my Father used always to read the morning service; and when in Delhi he was a most regular attender at the church there, going twice a day, even when he need not perform the service himself.

When we returned to Delhi after this visit to the Kutub, Uncle Edward and Aunt Mary had to leave us, to go to the station to which they had been appointed, Rohtuk, in my Father's division, which was fifty miles away. I missed their society very much, for as my Father was at office from ten o'clock to three every day, I often felt very lonely. The whole house was kept shut up all day during the hot weather, in order to keep out the heat and preserve what little coolness the night had brought, and the only things that broke the silence of all those hours were the occasional visits paid by the different members of society, as it was then the fashion to call before luncheon.

Sometimes I had to receive the young bachelor officers who called, and who had very few topics of conversation beyond those of local interest. Some of them called so often that I got to know the sound of the paces of their horses, and my Father and Aunt Mary used to be much amused to find that I always recognized the trot of the horse of a certain Captain Mainwaring, who had a very smart buggy and fancied himself very much. I have often wondered what became of that man. He belonged to the same regiment as Mr Lees. Other frequent callers were James Princep, a very pretty young man whose son married Evie Campbell, and a Mr Barford who wore

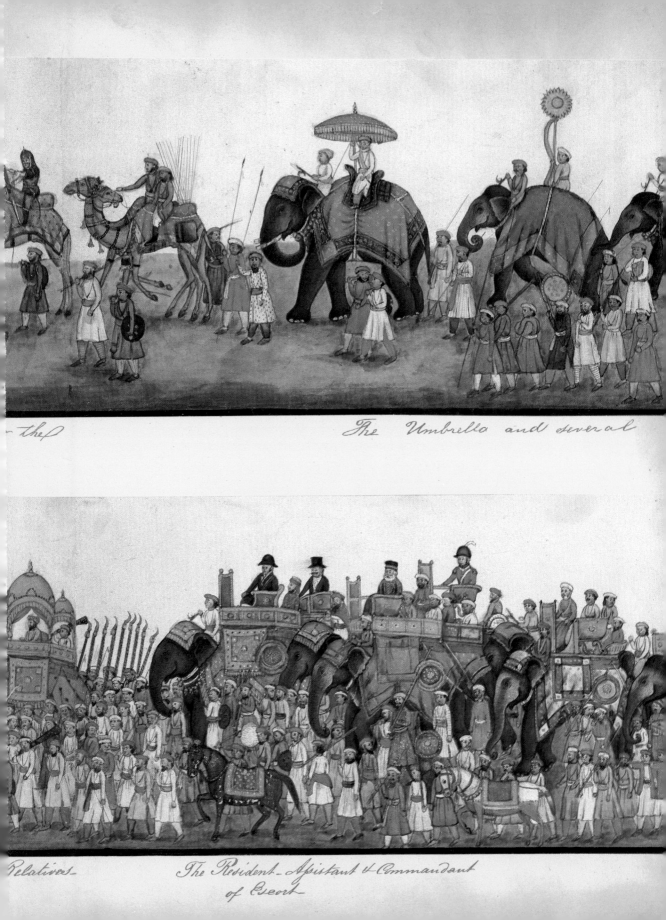

the

The Umbrella and several

Relatives

*The Resident - Afsistant & Commandant
of Escort*

e Ed=Gah or place of Sacrifice to celebrate the Festival of the Eed ool Koorban o
ded Sacrifice by Abraham of his son Isaac—

Heir Apparent Sons &c

"His Majesty the King of Delhie proceeding in full State
to the Ed-Gah or place of Sacrifice to celebrate the Festival
of the Eed ool Koorban or the Chief Sacrificial Festival.
It is in commemoration of the intended sacrifice by Abraham
of his son Isaac."

His Majesty the King of Dehlie proceeding in full State to
Chief Sacrificial Festival —   It is in Commemoration of the in

The Emperor

Sir Thomas Metcalfe is depicted in the Festival
Procession, seated upon an elephant with the Resident and the
Commandant of Escort, in the group immediately following
the Heir Apparent, Sons and Relatives.

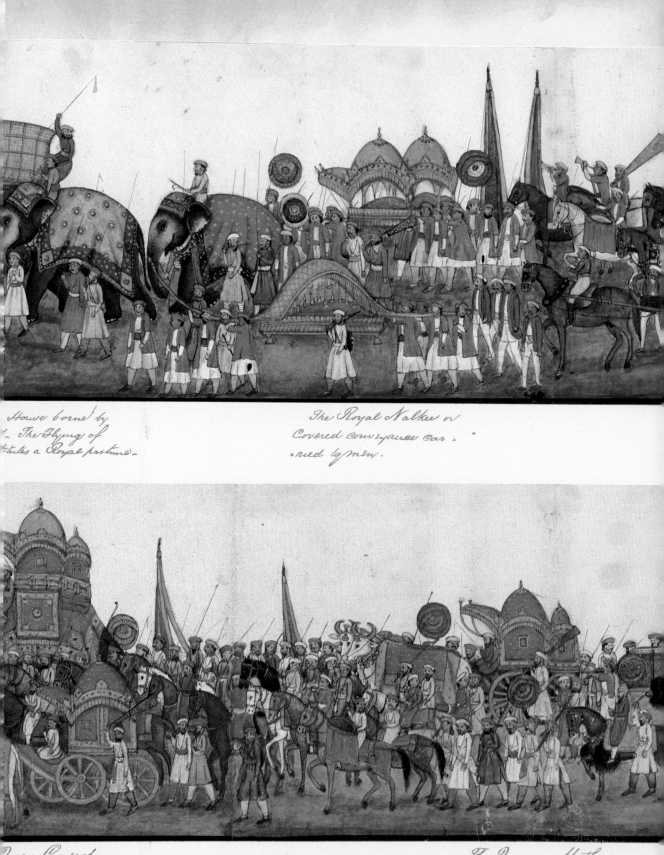

Howe borne by
...— The Flying of
...titutes a Royal posture—

The Royal Nalkee or
Covered conveyance car=
=ried by men.

Queen Consort.

The Queen Mother

Insignia of Sovereignty

The Pigeon
see Elephant
Pigeons, Cons[...]

The [...]

rings outside his kid gloves. These were both assistants under my Father.

Another assistant who came to Delhi in the course of that year was Gore Ouseley, such a jolly, happy-tempered boy, very clever, but he had never learnt to ride, and had therefore to begin this exercise at Delhi. He amused my Father and me by describing his progress in the art of riding by saying that he and his horse took simultaneous movements in contrary directions!

But in general they were very dull, and sometimes embarrassed me by making proposals of marriage, of which of course I informed my Father on his return from office. On one occasion a particularly ugly and impecunious youth had asked the all-important question, and when I told my Father, a quizzical look came upon his face, and fun to his eye, as he said: "And I suppose you have accepted him?"

There was plenty to amuse and interest me in looking over all the things in the house during the daytime, and I used to practice both harp and piano, and to read a good deal. But it was an exceedingly hot and trying season that first year – in fact, my Father said, one of the hottest he ever remembered – and I felt the heat dreadfully, notwithstanding the punkahs and thermantidotes and tatties that were at work to keep the house cool. The latter were of use only when a strong wind was blowing from the west, which was a very hot wind as it came from the desert of Sind to the west of Delhi. The tatties were screens about four inches thick, made of a sweet-scented grass called kuskus, and they were fitted exactly into one outside doorway in each room. A coolie was in attendance all day to throw buckets of cold water on to the grass from the verandah, so that when the west wind blew through it, it produced a cool breeze in the room, and the sweet refreshing scent pervaded the house. As all the doors and windows in the house were shut from seven o'clock in the morning until five in the afternoon, if the coolies did their work properly and the wind blew strongly, the house could be kept very cool as long as the weather was dry. But when the west wind ceased to blow, then the thermantidotes had to be resorted to. These were large wooden cases enclosed on three sides, but open on the front side, and fitted into a doorway, just as the tatties were. Inside the case was a wheel, which was turned by a long iron handle by a coolie in the verandah to produce the wind necessary to keep the house cool. There was a tattie in front of it so that the wind blew through it, and it was kept well watered. I used to sit as near to a

Royal Guards

Residents Escort from Skinner's Horse.

thermantidote or tattie as I could, so as to get all the cool air possible. Punkahs were also kept going in all the rooms that were occupied. Still the heat was terrific, and my Father was so anxious about my health that old Dr Ross was constantly sent for to look after me.

In those days there was no English chemist's shop at Delhi, and all the medicines were provided *gratis* by Government for the use of officers and civilians. There were none of the refined little arrangements in which we are accustomed to see medicines administered in England, and I was amazed and disgusted by getting a dose of senna sent me in a black beer bottle, and huge pills sent in a rough wooden box.

After our delicate homoeopathic treatment at Belstead (for Mrs Umphelby was quite in the van of progress in these matters) I felt quite shocked by such a coarse régime of medicine. On several occasions a large batch of leeches was also sent by Dr Ross to put on my side to cure the pain there. The result was that I was very soon pulled down to a condition of great weakness, and my Father was very uneasy about me.

The heat became so intense in May that the only cool times for a drive were three o'clock in the morning and nine o'clock at night. I used often to go out at the early morning hour, as I was glad to go to bed when my Father did at eight o'clock at night, being thoroughly exhausted by the heat.

Sometimes when it was a cooler evening than usual my Father would drive out with me in the carriage and we would go into the cantonments to hear the military band play. This was really the only social meeting of the society, and the carriages of the residents used to be drawn up round the band-stand, while the gentlemen passed from carriage to carriage to have a chat with the occupants.

At first I thought this rather fun, but I got soon tired of it, though I went occasionally for the sake of civility to meet acquaintances.

I have mentioned the subscription ball given at the Assembly Rooms to celebrate the Queen's birthday on May 24th, to which my Father took me, and he generally gave a dinner party once a month to twelve or sixteen people. This was given in the dining-room, where we dined every day, the large banqueting hall being used only for very large entertainments. My Father had beautiful plate and china, a good deal of the former inherited from his father, and the china that we used constantly would in these days have brought a fortune, for there were complete services of Derby, Worcester and oriental china. I little understood their value then, but only knew they were very handsome. There was so much plate that a great deal was kept locked up, and I was not the least aware of how much he possessed till the inventories had to be made after his death. Everything was solid silver, even the trays and saucepans, but it all went in the Mutiny.

Occasionally we had guests stopping in the house, and it was always a red letter day when Uncle Edward and Aunt Mary came to stay with us. My Father was not fond of going out to dinner in the hot weather, but sometimes he dined with the Gubbins' and Roberts', Rosses and Polwells, and the Robertsons at the Palace.

Mr and Mrs Arthur Roberts were both delightful people and very kind friends in those days, though we seldom met in after days. He was Judge at Delhi and greatly liked by my Father. One evening when we were dining with them in that hot weather of 1848 their little boy was standing by a table in the corner playing with some toys, when he called out: "Oh, Mama, tell this nasty thing to go away." On looking round Mr Roberts saw a cobra with its head raised standing in the corner of the room. He at once made a dash for it and fortunately killed it before it had time to injure anyone.

I used to enjoy driving through the streets of Delhi as everything was new and striking; the buildings of marble and red sandstone were so magnificent, the shops were so quaint, the colours of the cotton cloths hanging from the windows and across the streets were so gorgeous, the costumes so picturesque, and the crowds were so extraordinarily thick. Two syces rode at great speed in front of the carriage in order to clear the road, for the dashing little horses went at a good pace.

On fête days the crowd in the Chandnee Chouk, or Silver Street, was so numerous and compact that the children could walk on the heads of the people, which was an astonishing sight to anyone fresh from England. But alas! after the Mutiny, these crowds were no more to be seen. For some years afterwards only a few scattered groups of people were to be seen on gala days in this celebrated street, and although more inhabitants have now returned to Delhi, it can never be again what it was in those palmy days which I am describing.

Delhi was really a most beautiful city. It was surrounded by a magnificent wall of cut red sandstone, the top being crowned by a beautifully designed battlement. There were five or six very fine entrance gates, with fortifications to guard the approaches to the city.

The names of the chief gates were, the Cashmere Gate, the Cabul Gate, the Moree Gate, the Lahore Gate, the Calcutta Gate, and the Delhi Gate. There was also what was called the Water Gate of the city, situated close to the wall of the Palace by the river, but this was not as handsome as the others. It was through the small Water Gate that the mutineers entered Delhi on May 11th 1857, as the road from Meerut led to this entrance. [*In fact, it led to the Calcutta Gate, but that had been closed against them.* MMK]

The Cashmere Gate was the one nearest our house, and we passed through it every time we went into the city, as our house was situated about a mile outside the walls. It was through the Cashmere Gate that our troops stormed the city on the morning of September 14th 1857, and it was over a breach in the high wall near the gate that Uncle Theo led the way when the Light Infantry column rushed over it, the breach having been made by guns stationed at the stables in the grounds of Metcalfe House, which had been the foremost battery during the siege.

Emily's memory has led her a bit astray here. The Calcutta Gate was closed against the mutineers, but sympathizers among the Moghul's Court let them into the palace by one of the private entrances – probably the small Water Gate, which would have been the nearest one to the bridge of boats. The Kashmir Gate, to use the modern spelling, which Emily saw when it was as beautiful and as undamaged by time as when Shahjehan had it built, was battered and broken by the siege guns during the final assault on Delhi; a good deal of the damage being done by the guns commanded by my kinsman Edward Kaye, whose battery was one of the foremost ones. The inscription on the plinth marking its site reads:

No. II BATTERY – *Right,* [Commanding.] Major Edward Kaye, R.A.,	Armament	{ Two 18-pounders { Seven 8in howitzers To breach Kashmir Bastion.

In our day the *mali* used to keep his flowerpots and watering cans on it – although Bets and I always knew it was ours and not his, because it had our name engraved on it. The Gate itself, which has never been repaired, still looks as it did after the battle for the city. It is also certainly the nearest of Delhi's gates to the Metcalfe estate, and Emily's statement that the distance between them is only half a mile is reasonably accurate, since her father's land reached as far as the outer wall, now fallen, of the Kudsia Bagh. She could even be right when she says that the guns stationed in her father's stables were the "foremost battery during the siege", although they were definitely not the foremost during the assault. That was No. III Siege Battery on the edge of the Kudsia Bagh, with Edward Kaye's battery a close third, and "No. II Battery – *Left*" not much more than one hundred and fifty yards behind, in the grounds of Ludlow Castle. When I was last in Delhi the brick and sandstone plinths that mark the sites of all three of these batteries still stood, but I am afraid that by now the one on the edge of the Kudsia Bagh may have vanished, as a main road was in the process of being driven through those enchanted gardens of my childhood.

A broad moat ran all round the city at the foot of the wall, but it had not been flooded with water for many a long year, if indeed this had ever been done. After passing through the Cashmere Gate into the city, you found yourself in a walled enclosure, with an arcade running round it, which was used as a guardhouse, being always occupied by a guard of native soldiers under a European officer, the guard being changed once a week. Mrs Foster's house stood in a large enclosure next to the gateway, and then came the Magistrate's office, or Kutcherry, which overlooked the wall of the city with an extensive view across the river in the direction of Meerut.

It was from a window in this building that Uncle Theo looked out on the morning of May 11th and saw the mutinous cavalry riding along the road into Delhi, when he jumped into his buggy and galloped his horse hastily to the Calcutta Gate to close it, to prevent the entrance of the mutineers.

In the Magistrate's office was also the Treasury, where large sums of rupees were kept for the use of Government. A strong native guard was in charge of the Treasury, and it was to this place that Uncle Theo had sent his plate chest and a diamond tiara for safety during his absence from Delhi, as he was to have left Delhi and gone on leave to Cashmere that very night. But on the next day, May 12th, one of the King's sons came down to the Treasury, looted it of all it contained and carried off his spoil to the Palace.

The next house to the Treasury was a very pretty one in which my friends the John Gubbins' lived, and next to that was the office of the Delhi Press. In the large open space in front of these buildings was the English church, built at the sole expense of Colonel James Skinner, and it is in the churchyard surrounding it that my beloved Father was buried. There is also in this enclosure the grave of Mr William Fraser, who was murdered in Delhi in 1835, a circumstance I perfectly remember and to which I have referred.

There is a tablet to my Mother's memory in this church, and Colonel Skinner who built the church and who raised the regiment known as Skinner's Horse, is buried in the chancel. The church had then porticoes north, south and west, and was surmounted by a dome, with a gilt cross on the summit. The church was generally painted pink and was a strange piece of architecture, but it was well suited to the climate, and is full of sacred and happy memories to me. Here I was married on March 6th 1850, and Emmie was baptized there in the February following, and the funeral service for my Father was read here on November 4th 1853. 🙢

St James's Church – Skinner's church – has hardly changed at all from the picture that Sir Thomas Metcalfe had painted of it in the days when his friend James Skinner was still alive. The tablets that Emily mentions are still there, and anyone who visits the church today can see her father's grave and that of the "Commissioner and Resident of Delhi", the Honourable William Fraser, who was murdered on March 22nd 1835 – a day that Emily, then barely more than four and a half years old, was never to forget. The gilt cross and ball that surmounts the dome of the church is not the original one, for that became a favourite target with the mutineers, who did their best to shoot it down – and must have wasted a great deal of powder and shot in the process, since it was riddled with bullet-holes. After the Mutiny when the church, which had been sacked by the mob, was restored, this battered relic was taken down and replaced by a new one, the original being cemented into a marble plinth in the churchyard, with an engraved plaque explaining how it came to be there. Legend says that a number of the spent musket-balls were still inside it, and that could easily have been true. It stood there for almost ninety years, and was a familiar sight to churchgoers in Old Delhi. But within a few weeks of Independence it was stolen by hooligans – possibly for patriotic or merely anti-British motives – who probably destroyed it without realizing the historical value of such a relic. If anyone still has it, they could have a small fortune in their hands.

One can well understand the thinking behind the smashing and removal of relics left behind by an ex-conqueror. But people who do so would do well to remember that nowadays, when something belonging to the period of the Roman occupation of Britain is dug up by a bulldozer working on a new highway or the foundations for another block of highrise flats, the newspapers print columns about the find, a museum buys it and puts it on display, and hundreds of people stand in line to see it. Someday the same thing will happen to relics of the British Raj in India, and these too will be proudly displayed in museums, or treasured in private collections.

*O*n the opposite side of the church to the houses already described stood a palatial building called Skinner's House, the house of the numerous Skinner family, and adjoining it was a mosque built by Colonel Skinner for his Mohammedan friends.

Colonel Skinner was a man of dark blood, and his wife was a native lady, and their children were all, of course very dark in complexion, and spoke English with an extraordinary accent, and the whole family was a marvellous revelation to anyone fresh from England. Now it would be almost impossible to find a family of the same type in India, for although they looked upon themselves as English people and held a prominent position in Delhi society they had very little education and were more native than English in their ways.

My Father had a great regard for Colonel Skinner himself, as a warm-hearted friend and a very fine soldier, but it was difficult to say what the religion of the family was. I knew only two of the sons and one daughter. One son called Joe Skinner was a marvellous creation, as you may imagine when I tell you that his visiting dress consisted of a green cloth cutaway coat, with gilt buttons (or possibly gold as they were very pretty), very light claret-coloured trousers, patent leather boots, white waistcoat and gilt buttons, and a white necktie. He always carried a gold-mounted Malacca cane, with which he incessantly tapped his boot, and talked of the time when he was in the Guards, though he had never been out of India.

Another son was called Aleck Skinner, and when I went to call

upon his wife, who was supposed to be educated "English fashion",
she offered to sing to me, and thereupon sat herself down at the
piano and sang a song, playing the accompaniment herself; but both
words and tune were unknown to me until I looked at the title page
and found it was "Villikins and his Dinah", totally metamorphosed
by her playing and accent, and perfectly unrecognizable. 🐾

The song that Mrs Aleck Skinner played and sang was one of the great
Music Hall hits of the last century. It dates from the days when the
London cockney pronounced his "Ws" as "Vs" and *vice versa*. My father,
who had an inexhaustible fund of old Music Hall songs which my sister
and I found fascinating, numbered this one among his repertoire – I do not
know who had originally sung it to him; possibly one of his uncles? As far
as I remember, it tells the tale of poor Dinah whose hard-hearted father
would not allow her to marry her lover "Villikins", so the unhappy pair
committed suicide by drinking a "cup of cold pizen". (A sadder sight you
never "laid eyes on, than Villikins and his Dinah and the cup of cold
pizen"!)

With reference to Emily's following paragraph, we have to remember
that, to her, all Asians would have been considered "black", merely
because their complexions were darker than her own.

*T*his Aleck Skinner had a large family of sons and
daughters, who have, I suppose, succeeded to the large family
property. He sent me their photographs some time ago, and most of
them were named after the Royal Family, but they were all black.

To go back to a description of the city:

A fine broad road led to the King's Palace, which was surrounded
by another magnificent wall of cut red sandstone, with a battle-
mented top, and approached by a superb gateway at which always
stood a guard of native soldiers. High above this gateway and
approached by a long flight of steps were the rooms assigned to the
Assistant Resident, my Father's immediate subordinate, who was
supposed to keep a kind of surveillance over the Palace and to be at
hand if the King wished to make any urgent communication to him.
But alas! the proximity to the Palace was the cause of the murder of
all the inhabitants of those rooms on May 11th 1857. On that day 🐾

Captain Douglas, and my friend the Rev Mr Jennings and his daughter Margaret, who had been brought up with me at Belstead, and Miss Clifford, another visitor, were all murdered while sitting at breakfast in those rooms; and when I went there early in 1859 the splashes of blood were still on the walls. ✺

The Palace referred to stands inside the Lal Kila – the Red Fort that was built in Delhi on the orders of Akbar's son, the Emperor Shahjehan. The building was begun in 1638 and finished ten years later, and it became, as Emily says below, "a town in itself", since apart from the Emperor and his family and servants it housed also hordes of courtiers, ministers, scribes, musicians, dancing-girls and uncounted hangers-on, in addition to the Emperor's personal bodyguard, the permanent garrison, and a few shopkeepers. But it was intended as a fortress, with the palace built inside it for greater safety, and the complex is known not as the Palace of Delhi but as the Red Fort.

*T*he Palace itself covered an enormous space of ground; in fact it was quite a town in itself, thronged with thousands of natives, hangers-on of an oriental court.

Separated from the city by this great wall, it was open to the river all along one side of it, where sublimely beautiful buildings were erected, intermixed with gardens. Here were all the apartments devoted to the King of Delhi's harem, exquisite buildings of white marble, many of them inlaid with beautiful mosaics of different coloured stones, in the style of the Taj. Here also was the wonderful "Hall of Audience", the Dewan-i-Khas, than which a more beautiful building does not exist in the world. No picture can give an adequate idea of it, for in design, proportion, material and finish, it was faultless.

Floored and built entirely, inside and out, of polished white marble, it stood on a white marble terrace overlooking the river, and was a noble building, open on three sides and formed of exquisite arches, all inlaid with mosaics of cornelians and precious stones, with tracery in pure gold marking out the panels in different designs. It was erected for a Hall of Audience, where the great Moghuls of Delhi used to receive their subjects on state occasions. ✺

Continued au page 205

The Futtehpooree Mosque

نقشه مسجد فتح پوری دروازه لاهوری

was built by a female of that name in the service of the Emperor Shah Jahan who com-
-menced his reign A.D. 1628 (Page 8)— Two other Begums, Cotemporaries of the Futteh-
pooree also erected Mosques by desire of the Emperor and named them the Akburabadee &
Aurungabadee after themselves or rather from the places of their Birth by which they were designd.
Futtehpoor or the Town of Victory— Akburabad. the City of Akbur— and
Aurungab-ad. the City of the Throne.

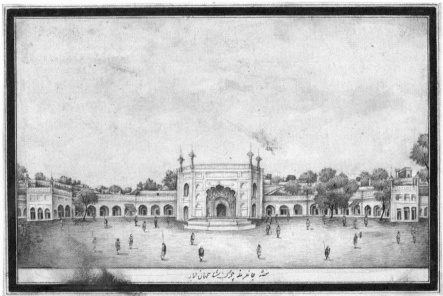

نقشه چاندنی چوک بازار خان آباد

The Chouk or Centre of the great Street, running in a direct
line from the Lahore Gate of the Palace to the above Mosque,
where it turns to the right, and is Continued to the Lahore Gate of the City—

The Citadel and Town of Toghluckabad, was built by the Emperor Gheeasoodeen Toghluck, the son of a Toorkee Slave. In A.D. 1321. the King Mobaruck Shah of the Khiljee Tribe was put to death by Khoosroo Khan an ungrateful favorite to whom the whole administration of the Government had been confided — On the death of the King, Khoosroo at once assumed the Vacant throne and murdered all the Survivors of the Royal Family — His sovereignty was but of short duration—for Ghouse Khan the Governor of the Punjab went into open Rebellion and marching to Dehly with the Veteran Troops of the Frontier, he gained a Victory over the dissolute and ill commanded Bands opposed to him and put an end to the Reign and life of the Usurper, to the universal joy of the People.

اینکه قلعه دهلی آباد

On entering Dehly Ghouse Khan made a declaration, that his only object was to deliver the Country from oppression, and that he was willing to place any of the Royal line on the Throne — No member of the Khiljee family was found to have Survived and Toghluck was himself proclaimed under the Title of Gheeasoodeen. His whole Reign was as commendable as his accession was blameless. He began by restoring order in his internal Administration and by putting his Frontier in an effective State of Defence — In A.D. 1324 = 5. the King proceeded in Person to to Bengal where Bohara or Boghra Khan the father of a former Emperor Keikobad still retained his Government after a lapse of 40 Years. He was now confirmed in Possession and permitted the use of Royal Ornaments by the son of his fathers former Slave.

The

The King also settled some disturbances in Dacca, then a Province independent of Bengal, and on his way back reduced Tirhoot and took the Raja Prisoner. As he approached his Capital in February of AD   , the Emperor was met by his eldest Son Fukhur oddeen Jonah Khan, who received him in magnificence in a wooden Pavilion erected for the occasion. During the Ceremonies the building gave way and the King with five other Persons was crushed on its fall.

The Misfortune may have been accidental, but, as before stated at Page 40 strong Suspicions existed that such was not the Case, more especially as Jonah Khan was absent at the time and that his next brother, who was the father's favorite was involved in the same Calamity.

The City of Toghluckabad is still remarkable for its extent and massive grandeur, and at its day, Cannon being unknown, it must have been impregnable. It was chiefly built of immense Masses of Stone raised one above the other to a considerable height and without Cement of any kind to connect them.

After the death of its Founder, it was not again the Seat of Empire. And on the introduction of our Rule in 1803, it was found to be the abode of Thieves who were the Terror of the Surrounding Country. By present Measurement the Ruins extend 3 miles in length and same in breadth. The Bastions are 61. and the Gateways 13 in number —

1 Aid of Religion.	6 A Turkish word.
2 Propitious. Fortunate.	7 A Proper name.
3 King.	8 Pride of the Faith.
4 A great King.	9 Old. Ancient.
5 Hero.	

بہشت منزل آباد سلطان عادل

The tomb of the Emperor Toghluck is connected with the Citadel by a causeway, and surrounded by beautiful Cultivation during the Spring Harvest.

The Durgah or Shrine of Shah Shurufoodeen[2], Boo[3]-Ulee Kulkiender[4], situated at Panneeputt about 50 Miles to the North of Dehly – Shurufoodeen was a native of Irak Babylon, and when about 42 Years of Age, accompanied his father to Dehly in the Reign of the Emperor Alla[5]oodeen Mushood Shah, who flourished A.D. , and established himself as a Professor of Languages and Theology, and there he continued for 20 Years – at this period of his Age, Tradition asserts that he was blessed by the Almighty in a Vision, and that throwing all his Books into the River and distributing his Worldly goods in Charity he became a Religious Devotee and for 40 Years travelled through the World and then again returned to Panneeputt. Allaoodeen Khibzee was now the reigning Prince A.D: 1311. and he at Shurufoodeen's Request, built the greater Portion of the Shrine at an Expence of 55000 Rupees or £5500 – Shurufoodeen died at Kurnaul A.D: 1324, and his immediate followers and disciples thought proper to enter his Remains at that place. As it is contrary to the Mohammedan Tenets to disinter a Body, his Relatives and friends who had intended that he should be buried at Panneeputt

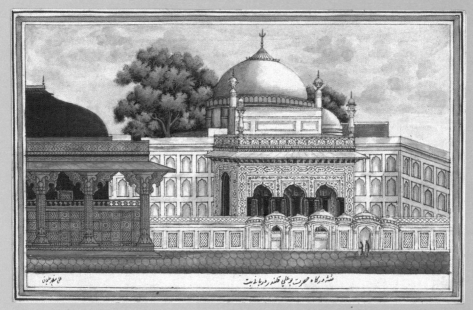

brought from Kurnaul with much solemnity a Brick taken from the Monument thence, and deposited it within the Sepulchre prepared for the Remains. It is however a disputed point to the present Day whether the Panneeputt or Kurnaul Shrine, contains the Remains. Two Villages yielding an Annual Revenue of Rs 4000 = £400 – were originally assigned for the Maintenance of the Shrine at Panneeputt, and the British Government now pay annually 2200 Rupees, on this account.

1 Literally King, but also applied to Holy men of great Sanctity
2 The Glory of Religion
3 No literal signification, also the name of a celebrated Physician long antecedent to the Subject of the present Memoir
4 A Description of Religious Devotee, corrupted in the English Translate of the Arabian Nights to Calender.

5 The Glory of Religion, corrupted into Aladin in the Story of the Wonderful Lamp, in the Arabian Nights.
6 Good Renown
7 Name of a Dynasty

The Principal Entrance to the Palace of Dehly and denominated the "Lahore Gate" from its face being in the direction of that Country. It looks towards the Chandnee Chowk or great Street of the City, in which is situated the Roshun ood Dowlah Mosque and Rotewals Chubootra. Vide page 12.13.

The second Principal Entrance to the Palace, and termed the Dehly Gate It faces nearly the Golden Mosque. Vide page 39.

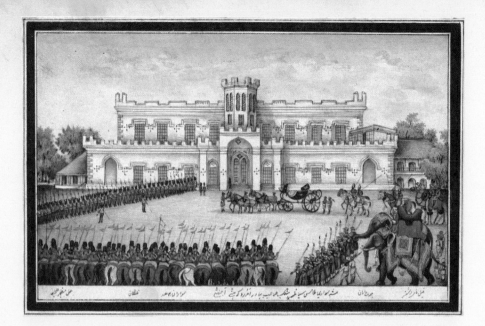

The Present Residence of the Agent to the Governor General,
with his retinue in attendance — The Building is also known
as "Ludlow Castle" having been built by S. Ludlow Esquire,
many years the Civil Surgeon of Dehlie — The proper
Residency hitherto in the occupation of the Chief authority
at Dehlie has lately been appropriated to the purposes
of an Anglo Indian College — greatly to the surprise of
the Native Community, and consequently in their
opinion somewhat to the discredit of the Ruling Power —

Elephant with Native Seat.

An Arab

سوار کابلی

A Native of Cabul

سنه پیل سوا پجم

The mosque attached to the Muidrussa or College, out side the City of Dehly

صورة مدرسه غياءالدين حيدر

Constructed by the Nawab Ghazeeoodein Khan (the defender of the Faith,) a distinguished nobleman in the Reign of Mohummued Shah and his Successor Ahmud Shah. Page 52.

He was the Father of the Individual of the same name who obtained the chief Power in the Reign and subsequently caused the Murder of the unfortunate Emperor Aulumgheire 2.d page 46.

مكتب خانه مقبره غياء الدين

South portion of the Interior of the Quadrangle

این عکس جائش فیروز علیاء الدین

The tomb also situated within the Quadrangle is of Marble and a very beautiful specimen of Dehly Art. It is said to contain the remains of the Founder: but the learned in these matters doubt the fact.

Ghazee oodeen it is well known died at Ahmedabad, in the Deccan, more than

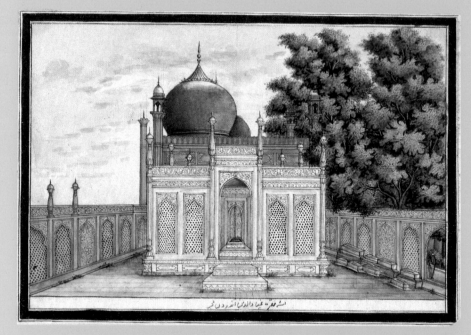

اسم عورت علیاء والدین اندرون نہر

400 miles from Dehly. But history also asserts that his remains were brought to the Imperial City – and if so – no Sepulchre could have been more fitting or more likely to be selected, than the one in Question.

The Tombs of the Newab Mohumud Umeen Khan and his son Kumroodeen Khan at Dehlie.

They were both natives of Toorkistan and came to Hindoostan during the reign of the Emperor Alumgheer Aurungzebe, who flourished between the years A.D 1658 and 1707 and on being presented at the Court of that Monarch, the former was honored with the Title of Khan, and raised first to the Command of 2000 and subsequently to that of 5000 Horse, a dignity of no Common order. which he con-

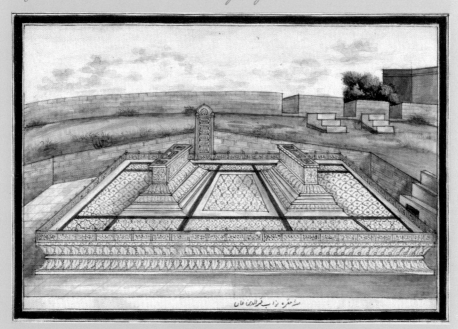

limued to enjoy until the reign of Furookh-Seer A.D 1713. when he was appointed Bukshee or Pay Master of the 2nd Grade — In the reign of the Emperor Mohumud Shah, Page 12, having succeeded in effecting the assassination of Hoosain Ullie Khan the Umeer ool Omrah, he was advanced to the dignities of Wuzeer or Prime Minister with additional Titles of higher order, and his son was appointed to the Pay Mastership vacant by his father's promotion —

Mohumud Umeen Khan died in A.D 1722 and after a short interval was

180

was succeeded in his Office by his son *Kumroodeen Khan* — The latter was killed in the action fought at *Sirhind* A.D. 1740 (Page 24) between *Ahmud Shah* the Afghan Ruler and the Emperor of *Hindoostan* of the same name. Both father and son are buried within the same Enclosure and Contiguous to the *Mudrussa* of *Ghazee oo deen Khan* (Page 64) The Tombs of both are beautiful though now much dilapidated. They were built by their respective Sons —

1. Praised.
2. Faithful.
3. Lord.
4. Light of the Faith.
5. Conqueror of the World.

6. Ornament of the Throne.
7. Of Happy or Virtuous habits.
8. Virtuous.
9. Chief of the Nobility.

Camel Artillery man, employed
also in carrying Expresses.

The Mobáruck Bágh

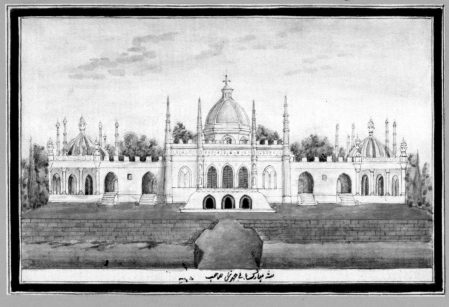

was constructed by the late Major General Sir David Ochterlong G.C.B– A most distinguished Officer, and talented Diplomatist–

It is believed that the portion of the building surmounted by the Dome was intended to form his Mausoleum– but as the General, demised at Meeruth, about 40 miles from Dehlie, his wishes could not be given effect to –

The Garden is situated about 4 miles to the North of Dehlie and much frequented during the Colder months of the year by parties from the Cantonments &c.

1.   Happy   2.   Garden

From the arrival of His Excellency Lord Lake in September 1803, the Tranquillity of Dehlie remained undisturbed until October 1804, when a body of Infantry detached from Holcars Army proceeded with a formidable Train of Artillery, invested the City and on the seventh of the above month, the siege commenced–

owing

Owing to a variety of pressing exigencies in other Quarters the Garrison at this time was not only too small for the defence of so immense a City, the Walls of which, besides their great extent, were accessible on all sides, but extremely faulty in its composition, consisting Chiefly of 300 Mewatters. robbers by profession- and a body of Irregular Horse, whose fidelity could not be relied on- The former justified their previous character by going over to the Enemy at an early period of the seige; and the Irregular Horse theirs, by flying at the approach of the Enemy, who in consequence approached close up to the Walls- Having opened their Batteries a few days afterwards, and several breaches being effected as much by the Concupions of the Guns on the Crumbling Ramparts as by the Enemy's fire- The latter made an attempt to carry the place by Escalade- In this they were repulsed and soon afterwards their Guns were spiked on their Batteries by a gallant and well conducted Sortie under Lieutt Rose, now Major General Sir John Rose K.C.B. of Home N. Britain-

Being thus baffled in all their endeavours they moved off on the 15th October, altho' they had prepared mines- By the judicious arrangements of then Co-lonel Ochterlony and Coll Burns, and the determined resistance of the Gar-rison, a small force was enabled to sustain a seige of nine days- repelled an assault. and defended a City nearly ten Miles in Circumference, which had ever been heretofore given up on the first appearance of an Enemy-

The Kutb or Kootub Minar, distant about 12 miles from Dehlie SW. is said to have been completed in the reign of Shumsodeen Altumsh (AD. 1211) one of the Toorki Slave Kings — In Elphinstone's India the height is stated at 242 feet — by the late Major General Mackenzie, the highly talented Surveyor General — the original height was Computed at 269 feet. It rises on five stages with projecting Galleries at Each. The lowest three are of red Stone, the 4th of red stone intermixed with Marble — The first story, Height 90, is formed of 27 Divisions or Compartments, alternately Semi Circular and angular — The 2d St. 50 of semi-circular only — and the 3d St. 40 of Angular ones. Three hundred and Seventynine is believed to be the Correct number of Steps —

On the night of the 10th September 1803. the eve of the Battle of Dehlie, the Pillar was seriously injured by an Earthquake and more especially at the base and 3d Story — the latter of which Bulges Considerably. it was subsequently 1826/27 repaired by the British Government at an expense of Rs. 20,000 or £2000 —

It is believed to be the highest Column in the world, and in an Inscription it is ascribed to Shahabodeen Ghoree, who invaded India in 1193 — by others to Kootubodeen — the Slave and afterwards the regal representative of the former in India — Both Mahomedans and Hindoos assert a national claim thereto — In favor of the former the Koran Inscriptions are Evidenced — and Tradition sup- -poses that the Column was intended as a Minaret to a Mosque of which the three beautiful arches now in ruins, and the uncompleted Minar at a distance were to form Component parts — but the last mentioned is 1/3d larger in Circumference and is raised on a base, which is wanting in the present Pillar

and

نقش مینار حاجیہ جامع مسجد قطب الدین صاحب

نقش مینار جامع مسجد ویہ مینارہ

and moreover the Entrance door way is on the East side, all right and proper, whereas in the latter you enter on the North Side, a most unusual arrangement in a Mohumudan Building. it is therefore Clear the two were never built to Correspond—

The immediate Environs of the Kootub are known to have formed the old Hindoo City of Delee; from the Zemindar of the place. and from which our Dehlie is derived— and there still exist numerous Specimens of the most primitive Hindoo Architecture— Could not the unfinished Column have been Commenced by the Faithful on a larger Scale to outdo the Idolaters, and failing to perfect the work, Could not the Koran Inscriptions have been added to the Pillar—

The 2nd and unfinished Pillar
above alluded to

The Tomb of the Emperor Shumsood deen, Altumish situated at the Kootunb.

It is related of Altumish though probably not until after his Elevation to the Throne in A.D: 1211, that he was of Noble Family and being like Joseph in his youth the favorite of his father and thereby envied by the rest of his Brothers, they stripped him one day when Hunting and sold him to a Company of travelling Merchants. The latter carried him to Bokhara and sold him to one of the Relatives of the Prince of the Country, under whom he received a liberal education.   On the death of his Master he was again exposed to Sale and purchased by a Merchant who sold him again to another who carried him to Ghuznee.   The Emperor Mohummed Ghoree heard of Altumish's beauty and Talents but could not agree with the Merchant about his Price. he was therefore carried back to Bokhara as none durst buy him on account of the King's displeasure 'till Kootooboodeen (the Pole Star of Religion) alluded to at Page 74. obtaining the King's Permission, purchased him at Dehly whither he had invited the Merchant owner, for 50 thousand pieces of Silver. Subsequently Kootooboodeen gave Altumish, his second Daughter in marriage.
As the Son in Law of his Master, Altumish rose in Rank until he was created Tenurab in

Chief, and on the death of his father in law, he advanced against the Capital, expelled "Aram", his Brother in Law and Son of his Benefactor from the Throne and declared himself King with the Title of Shumsoodeen Altumish.
Shumsooddeen signifies the Sun of Religion and Altumish is the Turkish word for Sixty and conferred or assumed from the Circumstance of his having been purchased for Sixty Toomuns.
On his accession he was acknowledged by many Chiefs and Princes, but some of his Generals taking offence went off with the greater part of his Toorkee Horse, the flower of his Army. These connecting themselves with other Malcontents, advanced to the Capital of Dehly where they were opposed by Altumish and defeated. Their Chief Furrookh (Propitious) was slain in the Field, and the rest so closely pursued, that in a short time, they were all either killed or taken, which established Altumish on the Throne.
All Hindoostan, save some insulated Portions were made from time to time to acknowledge the government of Dehly: but the obedience of the different Portions
was

was in different degrees. From entire Subjection to very imperfect Independance.

After these Successes Altumish returned to Dehly and died in April 1236 - after a Reign of 26 Years, as he was about to depart on a Journey to Mooltan - He was an Enterprising, able and good Prince, and during his Reign, he received Investiture from the Caleph of Bagdad. the most Authoritative Recognition of a new Government that could take place among Mohummedans.

"His Wuzeer or Minister towards the latter end of his Reign was" Fukheer ool Moolk (the Pride of the State) who had formerly been Minister to the Caleph of Bagdad for 30 Years, whence he was much esteemed on account of his Wisdom and Learning.

The Beautiful Column of the Kootoob is said to have been completed in this Reign.

The same Tomb as the above, but in a different View and by a different Artist.

The Shrine of Jog Maya at the Kootoob dedicated to Devee an Hindoo Goddess is said to have been from time immemorial the Site of Idolatrous Worship. The two Temples represented were built, the one by Rana Peertie or Pritzy Raj. and the other by his Chief Almoner — Rana Peertee called also Rae Pittorah, the latter a Corruption without any meaning, was the King of Ajmeer and Indra Put⁴, the ancient Hindoo City of Dehly, the name being derived from Dellee or Dehlee, the Chief Zemeendar or Land Proprietor of the Place.

It was in Pittorah's Reign that the Afghan Emperor Shuhabooddeen Ghoree (Vide page 74) invaded India. In his first Expedition A.D 1186, he took possession of Lahore — He next turned his Arms against the Hindoo Princes of Hindoostan, but was defeated in his first attempt by Rae Pittorah in A.D: 1191 at Telowree, one march from Kurnaul: but in 1193, he again returned with an immense Army. Pittorah was in his turn defeated and being taken Prisoner in the pursuit was put to Death in cold blood.

Since the introduction of the British Rule, the Shrine has been much enlarged and Beautified by the Hindoo nobility of Dehly — It is held in much Repute by Idolators and at annual Periods is visited from afar by thousands of misguided Devotees who liberally according to their several means present Offerings to the Goddess and make vows of future Pecuniary Sacrifice on the fulfillment of their Hopes or Prayers

1	Worship.	7	King
2	Wealth. also a name for Luchmee the Goddess of Wealth.	8	God of Elements
3	King - Chief.	9	Town or City
4, 5, 6	Peertie or Pritvy Raj. Lord of the Earth.	10	Strength of the Faith
		11	Name of Family or Dynasty

The Houz Shumshee or Reservoir of Light.

A very beautiful Lake. During the heighth of the Rainy season of each year, situated about two Miles from the Kootoob Pillar is said to have been constructed by the Emperor Shums'oo deen Altumish [2] (vide Page 75-b) from whence its name. Idle tradition asserts that Water being very Scarce at the Place, the Emperor in a dream received a Communication from the Prophet Mahomet directing him to search for the foot Mark of his, the Proph'ts Horse and there to dig. This we are expected to believe was successfully attended to.

1   Light of the Faith.
2. Sixty. The Emperor having been purchased as a Slave for Sixty pieces of Silver —

190

The Tomb of Mohummud Hossain – Paie Meenar commonly called Imaum Zamin.

The two first words give the name of the individual. the two second signify that he was interred at the foot of the Pillar. The two last were distinguished appellatives conferred on an Ancestor and by Courtesy continued to the Descendant.

The Subject of the Memoir was originally of Meshed, a celebrated City of Khorasan, and came to Hindoostan in the time of the Emperor Mohummud Shah Adili, who usurped the sovereignty in A.D. 1553. on the death of his nephew Suleem Shah

the Son of Shere Shah (vide page). He was much famed for his Sanctity and held in high Estimation by the Emperor. He died after the Restoration of the Emperor Hoomaeon (vide page 9) to the Throne of Dehly. and the Mausoleum was erected by the Emperor Ukbur the Great over the spot in which his Remains had been deposited and where he had passed the last Years of his life in Religious Seclusion.

1 Praised. also the name of the Prophet.'
2. Virtuous
3 Foot
4 Pillar

5. Priest. Leader in Religious Ceremonies
6 Surety. a Sponsor – literally. Responsible for the Religious Tenets delivered by him.
7 Foot

The Tomb of Khwájeh Kooloob obd deen¹ is situated at the Rootoob and held in much Veneration by all Classes of Mohummudans. This saint for so he is considered was a native of Persia. When Young he devoted himself to Religious Exercises and was greatly favoured by Lights from above.

When 18 Years of Age, he visited India during the Reign of Shumsood deen Altumish³ page 76. and took up his abode at Dehly. and soon became a popular Teacher.

In A.D: 1236. during a religious Assembly, he was so Transported by the recital of some Verses of a pious nature that he became suddenly entranced and in this state expired.

The Tomb which is of the cheapest Material, was constructed by a disciple of the deceased. The Mosque seen on the background was built by the Holy Man himself. Emperors from Molvies

درگاه قطب

of piety have enlarged and ornamented the Shrine. Many persons of great Sanctity or of high rank have been interred within the Precincts. Amongst the latter, the Emperor Shah Aulum and his Son the late King Uckbur the 2d. A Village in the neighborhood, yielding an annual Revenue of Rupees 2,000m. or £200, was assigned by the Kings of Dehly for the Expense of the Shrine. and the same indulgence has been continued by the British Government.

1. Preceptor. Teacher   4. Sixty.
2. Pole Star of Religion   5. King of the World.
3. Light of Religion

The Iron Pillar at the Kootoob is said to have been erected by Rana Pirthee Raj commonly called Rae Pittorah Page 77. He succeeded to the Throne about A.D. 1131, Fifteen Years afterwards he defeated Shahaboodeen Ghoree on his first invasion of India. He was equally successful a short time afterwards in a contest with the Raja of Kanouj, on which occasion he erected this Pillar as a Trophy.

Tradition states that the Soothsayers of the Court represented to the King that if the Pillar were sunk in a particular spot it would rest on the head of a serpent, and that until it was removed, the King's Dynasty would remain on the Throne. The proper Site was selected but the King less superstitious than his Men of Oracles subsequently directed the Pillar to be taken up with a view to ascertain, if as was asserted, the end of the Shaft would be found to be stained with the Blood of the Victim.

Such is said to have been case, and the Pillar was immediately recommitted to the Earth, but it had once been removed, the charm was broken, and soon after Shahaboodeen Ghoree again invaded India and Rae Pittorah and his Dynasty passed from the Earth.

This very singular Pillar is situated near to the Kootoob Meenar, and is about ____ feet in height, and those deeply learned in antiquarian Lore records their Belief that its length is as great below as it rises above the Earth.

The Jhurna or Waterfall at the Kootoob.

املہ چھیرنہ ارقطب

Constructed during the Reign of the Emperor Mohummed Shah (Vide page 12) who
reigned between the Years A.D 5719 & 1748 – It is much resorted to by the present
King and the Ladies of his Family, and is supplied from the Howz Shumshee
described at Page 77.

The Tomb of Udhum Khan, who having assassinated his Foster
Brother, (see Page   ) attempted also the life of the Emperor Ack:
bur the Great by whose orders he was thrown from the Battlements
of the Palace.

The Name is generally pronounced so like your Adam, that new
arrivals are sometimes made to believe that the Building is really
the Tomb of our common Progenitor.

مزه مشاه عبد الحق دهلوی

The Tomb of Shaikh Ubdool¹ Huq² Dehlevee.³ the ancestor of this individual was a native of Bokhara, but on Visiting Dehly was ennobled and attached to the Royal Court. The father obtained a great name for sanctity: the son (who was born at Dehly) followed in his parent's footsteps and made two Pilgrimages to the holy Mecca. He died in the Reign of the Emperor Shah⁴ Juhan A.D. 1642. and was buried in the Sepulchre built by himself on the Margin of the Lake Houz Shumshee, described at page 77.

1 Tribe: Caste.
2 Slave of God.
3 of Dehly
4 King of the world

The Tomb of the Emperor Shah 'Alum at the Kootub — Ullee Gohur for such was
his real name, was the eldest son of Alumgeer 2.d who was assassinated in 1759 by his Mi-
-nister Ghazeeoodeen Khan Page 46 — As Heir Apparent he had been previously compelled to
fly from Dehlie, and as nominal Emperor he commenced his reign by an unprovoked and ill
conducted attack on the British in Bengal and Behar then recently acquired by the latter — but
finding himself Baffled and defeated, he soon after voluntarily surrendered himself in the British
Camp, without treaty, Condition or stipulation — In his absence from the Seat of Government, another Member of the Royal Family was raised to the Throne by the Regicide, but this Prince's Title was
never acknowledged —

The Mahratta power was at this time at its Zenith — the Military Establishments had increased
with its power, and its force now included an army of well paid and well mounted Cavalry and 10,000

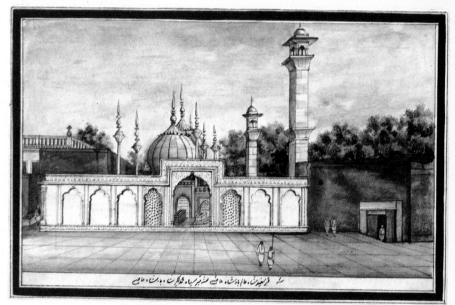

ستہ قبر حضرت غازی بادشاہ عالم شاہ قبر در پیش ....

disciplined Infantry superior to any Infantry previously known in India —

About A.D. 1769 The Mahratta Chief Sudasheo Bhow captured Dehlie. He made an ungene-
rous use of his Conquest. defaced the Palaces Tombs and Shrines for the sake of the rich ornaments
which had been spared by the Afghans and Persians — tore down the Silver Ceiling of the Hall of
Audience. page 20. which was coined into 17 Lacks of Rupees equal to £170,000, and seized on the
Throne (no longer however precious, as of old) and on all other Royal ornaments — Years of anar-
chy and oppression succeeded the death of the unfortunate Alumgeer the 2.d — at last Ullie
Gohur under the title of Shah Alum, was enabled Chiefly by the assistance of Shooja oo
Dowlah to return to Dehlie, and on the 25th December 1771 A.D. made his Entry into the
Capital with much pomp and splendor and amidst the acclamations of all ranks of people —

In

In 1765 a Pension of 26 Lakhs of Rupees 260,000£ had been settled upon him annually by the British Government with a considerable Tract of fertile Territory in Upper Hindostan both of which he forfeited on quitting the protection of his Benefactors and repairing to Dehlie, became a Prisoner and Political Instrument under the Custody of the Mahrattas —

In 1788 Goolaum Kaudur the Rohilla having by a sudden eruption made himself master of Dehlie, seized the unfortunate Emperor, and after exposing him for many weeks to every species of insult and degradation in order to extort the disclosure of supposed concealed Treasures, concluded by piercing his eyes with a dagger so as completely to extinguish sight. For the attainment of the same object he massacred, starved to death, and tortured many of the Royal Family and of the Chief inhabitants of Dehlie, but being compelled to evacuate the City by a detachment from the Mahratta Army, he was captured during his flight and expired under the effects of even greater Tortures than he had so mercilessly inflicted —

Nor was the misery of the Mogul Emperor much alleviated by the Transfer, which about this period took place, of Dehlie, and some adjacent Territory from the Mahratta Chief to the French Officers commanding the Corps of disciplined Infantry retained in the Service of the Chief, for tho' the King was ostensibly under the Superintendance of those Officers, he yet effectually remained a Prisoner in the hands of the Mahrattas and subjected to all their proverbial rapacity —

During the year 1802 when there were 52 sons and daughters of the Emperor the monthly stipend allowed to each Prince of the Imperial Family did not exceed 15 Rs per month (21£ per annum) and the sums disbursed by the French Officer who had charge of the Emperor's person, for the aggregate Expenses of His Majesty — the Royal Family — Dependants and Establishments amounted only to 1700 Rs per month or £23,664 per annum, while the Mahrattas retained and converted to their own use all the Gardens and Houses, in or about the City that were Royal property and perpetrated the most atrocious Crimes, in the name of their Royal Prisoner for the purposes of Fraud and Extortion —

Such was the desolation of this ancient Capital, in 1803, when Lord Lake having defeated the Mahratta Army six miles from Dehlie on the 11th September & entered it the next day to the infinite Joy of the Aged Emperor. and from this time the British Jurisdiction has continued Supreme — Shah Aulum closed a long and Calamitous reign of 43 Years in December 1806, in the 85th year of his life — and on the same day was succeeded by his Eldest legitimate son Akbar the 2d the late Emperor —

1. King of the World.
2. Glorious
3. Race.
4. Conqueror of the World.
5. Star of the Faith.
6. Name of Hindoo Deity
   Sikh or Siva the Destroyer

7. Literally "approved".
8. The most valiant of the State.
9. Literally "Slave".
10. Powerful.
11. Name of a Tribe.

The Tomb of the Emperor Naser'oodeen Mohummud at the Kootoob. commonly known by the name of Sooltan Ghazee.

By the Honorable Mr Elphinstone he is said to have been a grand son, and by native Historians the son of the Emperor Shumsoodeen Ultumish, page   ; He was imprisoned immediately on his father's death, and tho' he had been some time Released and entrusted with a Government, he retained the Retired and studious habits of his youth. He succeeded his grand Nephew, the Emperor Alaoodeen, who after a Reign of two Years of Cruelty and licentiousness was deposed and put to death A.D. 1241. The twenty years Reign of Naseroodeen. was full of Disturbances foreign and domestic, though none sufficient to overturn his Government.

He at first reposed implicit Confidence in his Minister Gheeas'oodeen Bulbeen

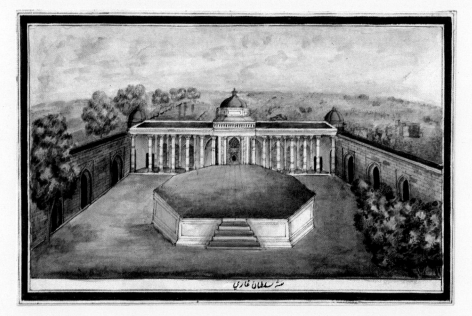

مش سلطان غازی

whose measures were eminently successful, and although the King accompanied the Army and was the ostensible author of all its Military Success, he nevertheless began to feel uneasy in the secondary place which he really occupied, and was induced by the insinuation of an artful Courtier Imad'oodeen, who had risen by the favor of the Minister to remove the latter from his post, and confer it on his secret accuser.

All the Ministers immediate adherents were also soon displaced. The Misgovernment which followed created extensive discontents and Remonstrances were addressed to the King demanding the dismissal of the new Minister.

Gheeas'oodeen was recalled, and henceforth became the real Head of the Government. Imadoodeen A.D. 1215, raised a Rebellion, in which he involved a relation of the King, and though he was soon taken Prisoner and put to Death, the Rebellion was not quelled till the end of the second Year.

In A.D. 1258, it was found necessary to put down the inhabitants of Mewat a brave and turbulent Race of Mountaineers, to the South of Dehly, and tho' not distant more than 25 Miles, it was not without great exertion and some Danger that the King defeated them in battle and ultimately reduced this Country. Ten thousand of the insurgents are said to have been slain.

This predatory tribe were never entirely quieted until the Establishment of the British Government.

. The Emperor died a natural death in February A.D. 1266. His private life was that of a Dervice. He defrayed all his personal Expence by copying Books. His fare was of the humblest description and was cooked by the Queen. to whom he allowed no female Servant. He was an eminent Patron of Persian Literature; and a general history of Persia and India, a work of the highest Celebrity was written at his Court.

He was succeeded by his Minister Gheeasooden Bulbun.

1 Defender of the Faith	5 Glory of Religion
2 Name of the Prophet.	6 Aid of Religion
3 Emperor.	7 Proper name no meaning
4 From Shar a Caveon. the emperor having directed that he should when dead be thrown into a Hole	8 Pillar of Religion

of a quiet little Residence at the Kootoob, as yet unhonored by
a name. prettily situated and of convenient access whenever
retirement or change of Air is desirable. It is but yet in its infancy. a few
months will, I trust perfect both its comfort and Beauty

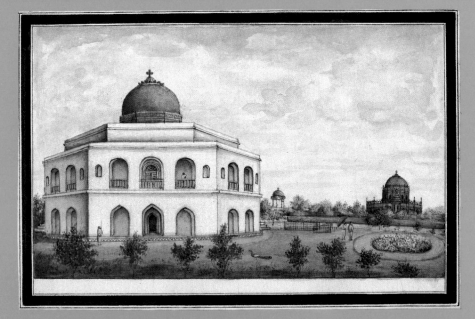

The North West View, with the Tomb of Udhum Khan (vide Page 80) in the
Distance. ——————

Plan of the House at Lehlee

a Study
b Library
c Napoleon Gallery
d Principal Dining room
e Drawing room
f Hall

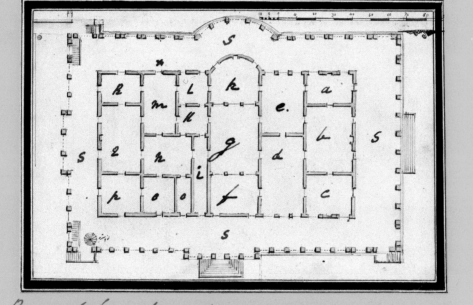

g - Breakfast & dining room
h - Bay room - Winter Breakfast room
i - Passage - K. Ante room
L Prayer room -
m - My dressing room * The door by which Fua Lamen
    = led Mother left the House for the last time
    at 9 o'clock of the Evening of 2nd May 1842.
n - Strangers room - o-o - Bathing rooms.
s. Your Mothers dressing room & the nursery - and will be
   Emelys room when she joins me - q Your Mothers
   favorite Sitting room - R. Bed room - S.S Verandahs

To You my very dear Children

Front View
West

منه کوشش ملازم الدولہ والدین ظفرجنگ قطام یار خان نریدہ احمد سلطانی طاسی کا ملاں قشنگ طاہر صاحب جلاد و بندرو ظفاہ

These Mementoes cannot fail to be of more Common
Interest, – In this once happy Home you ale passed
Your Earliest Infancy – with Exception to Emy and
Charley ale were born here – and ale but Charley-
here received the initiatory Right of Baptism
by which We were made members of Christ
Children of GOD – and Inheritors by Promise
of the Kingdom of Heaven — To Your Father
It has been Endeared by many Years of more

Back View
East

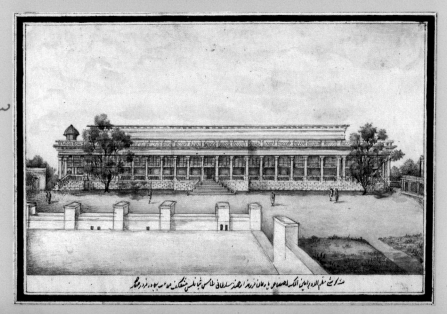

منہ کوشش ملازم الدولہ والدین الکرہ الصدیق یار خان نریدہ احمد سلطانی طاسی ملاں قشنگ طاہر صاحب جلاد و بندرو ظفاہ

Principal Tek-Khanah or under Ground Apartment occupied, during the Hottest month of the year

than usual Happiness and now rendered Sacred by the memory of Her whose Many Virtues Devoted Affection and pious resignation under Trials and affliction were then but imperfectly appreciated

Strive my Beloved Girls during your Pilgrimage on Earth, to imitate the Example of Your Sainted Parent, that you may Hereafter be deemed worthy, through the Intercession of our Saviour, of being reunited to her, for all Eternity in the Many Mansions of our Fathers House.

Second Tek-Khanah used as a Billiard Room —

مشتقدار و بردار

View from the East side of the House, in-
-cluding the Palace- the Great Mosque.
St James' Church-

There was a great block of crystal at one end of the hall on which the famous Peacock Throne once stood – the golden chair of state from which rose a magnificent ornament representing the feathers of an outspread peacock's tail, every feather being encrusted with precious stones of enormous value, the Koh-i-noor being one of them.

When Emily talks of "mosaic" she does not mean what we mean by that word – pictures made up of small pieces of coloured marble or glass. These were designs inlaid into the marble, much of the material used being semi-precious stones: crystal, lapis-lazuli, Jaipur-jade and rose-quartz, jasper, cornelian, onyx, turquoise, beryl and blood-stone. At one time jewels of even greater value were probably used – diamonds, emeralds, rubies and sapphires. But these would have been looted long ago, if not by the Persian invader Nadir Shah then by Ahmad Shah Durrani; both of whom sacked Delhi, the latter with the aid of the Jats of Bhurtpore.

It was Nadir Shah who looted the famous Peacock Throne and took it back with him to Persia, and a great deal of it must still be there – although in bits and pieces and no longer as a whole, for successive Shahs of Persia have removed and reset most of the jewels and melted down a great deal of the gold. I am aware that the experts say that the Koh-i-nur diamond, the "Mountain of Light" was part of the jewelled throne, but I can never quite believe this, since if it was, Nadir Shah certainly took it, along with the rest of the throne, and I should like to know how it then came to be in the possession of the Amir of Afghanistan – from whom Ranjit Singh, the "Lion of the Punjab", stole it by a trick while the Amir was his guest.

The tale goes, and it is a true tale, that Ranjit learned from some spy in the Afghan ruler's retinue that the Amir was so afraid of losing the diamond that he always carried it with him, hidden among the folds of his turban. So during one of the banquets given by the "Lion" to celebrate the signing of a treaty between them, the host insisted on exchanging turbans with his honoured guest as a sign of friendship. The poor Amir being unable to refuse (since to do so would have been a deadly insult), Ranjit got the Koh-i-nur. But when the Sikhs were later defeated by the British, the great diamond became a prize of war, and was sent as such to Queen Victoria, who had it cut from 268 carats to 186, to enhance its brilliance. (When mined, it is supposed to have weighed 756 carats – a mountain of light indeed!)

To give you some idea of the enormous riches of the Moghul court, the famous Peacock Throne, which originally incorporated two peacocks, stood on four feet of solid gold frosted over with diamonds, rubies and emeralds in the form of a jewelled aigrette, and was valued, at that time, at four and a half million pounds (the imagination boggles at what it would be worth now!). A gentleman named Tavernier, a professional jeweller who saw it in 1665, described it as being six feet by four and shaped like a bed, supported by four gold feet from twenty to twenty-five inches high. Three gold steps led up to the throne, which was decorated with 108 rubies and 116 emeralds, while twelve columns set with rows of large pearls supported the canopy; these last, in Tavernier's opinion, were the most valuable part of the throne. The canopy itself was fringed with pearls and covered on the inside with hundreds of diamonds and pearls, and on its four-sided dome stood a peacock whose tail was "made of sapphires and other coloured stones, the body being of gold inlaid with precious stones, having a large ruby in front of the breast, from whence hangs a pear-shaped pearl of fifty-six carats or thereabouts, and of a somewhat yellow water".

On the front of the canopy glowed a great diamond surrounded by emeralds and rubies – this was supposed to be the Mountain of Light – and flanking the throne stood two tall red velvet umbrellas embroidered and fringed with pearls, their eight-foot sticks thickly studded with diamonds, rubies and pearls.

All this splendour formed only one of the many items that Nadir Shah took back with him to Persia, so his total loot must have been fabulous. Yet when Delhi was sacked again only seventeen years later the loot taken from it on that occasion was almost as stupendous. I have seen one item of it myself, and it literally took my breath away.

Of course I never saw this Peacock Throne, as it had been looted by Nadir Shah in 1739. But the block of crystal remained, on the top of which luxurious cushions of cloth of gold used to be spread for the King to sit on when receiving his subjects. In four of the panels above the arches and just below the ceiling, which was of white marble inlaid with gold, were beautifully engraved Persian words inlaid in gold, the translation of which was:

If there be a Paradise upon Earth,
It is this, it is this, it is this.

This inscription suggested to Thomas Moore the lines in "Lalla Rookh".

The bathing establishments for both the King and the ladies of his family were all of white marble, the walls being inlaid with the same beautiful mosaics.

The Dewan-i-Khas, or Hall of Audience which I have just described, was screened from the King's private apartments by means of white marble so elaborately pierced that its traceries appeared just like lacework. Behind this hung curtains of richest silks to ensure privacy, but which allowed the old Queen to hear everything that was going on in the public audiences.

Outside the arches there were curtains of brilliant red cloth, which could be either raised or lowered according to the weather.

This superb building still exists, as fortunately it was not materially injured in the siege, but many of the mosaics were thoughtlessly spoilt by the soldiers with their bayonets, when it was taken possession of after the siege, and used as a church by the regiments occupying the Palace.

I am very much afraid that the spoiling of what Emily calls "the mosaics" cannot be put down to "thoughtlessness", but was done deliberately by soldiers who prised out the leaves and petals of the beautiful, inlaid flower patterns with the points of knives and bayonets, under the impression that the stones they were removing were valuable jewels and could be sold for large sums of money. They also, almost certainly, removed every scrap of gold inlay from the ceiling – and anywhere else! – for the golden plates on the domes of the lovely pearl mosque were not the only gold that had been lavished on the decoration of the palace. And as you can see from Tavernier's description of the Peacock Throne it is not surprising that the ordinary soldier in the ranks was convinced that these bits of coloured stone and marble must be jewels of great price – which considered as works of art and taken as a whole they were: and are! For much of the damage has been carefully repaired, and the Diwan-i-Khas is still one of the loveliest buildings in the world, while the Palace is probably more beautiful without the garish Peacock Throne than it was in the days of its greatest fame and opulence. I do not know what has happened to the great block of crystal that Emily describes – I cannot remember ever seeing it myself.

*T*here was another Hall of Audience in the centre of the Palace, which was used for ordinary occasions, when the King sat to give judgement or hear petitions. This was not nearly so beautiful in the materials used, although the architecture was in the same style, and on these occasions the King sat in a kind of opera box, large enough to hold him and a few of his attendants. In the walls of this opera box were some beautiful Italian mosaics in the Florentine style, executed by Italians in the seventeenth century. They consisted principally of different kinds of birds and flowers, but one larger one about a foot high represented Orpheus with his lute playing to animals at his feet. These mosaics of course belonged strictly to the Government, but this large one was taken out of the wall as loot by an officer commanding one of the English regiments, and afterwards *sold* as his private property to the India Office in London, who deposited it in the South Kensington Museum. [*Paintings of the mosaics are shown on pages 70–73 of the "Delhie Book".* MMK]

One of the most beautiful buildings in the Palace, indeed in all India, was the Pearl Mosque, a small white marble mosque erected for and used by the ladies of the King's household. The entire mosque and courtyard and surrounding walls were all of beautiful white marble, highly polished, and the mosque itself had all its arches and interior inlaid with gold tracery, and was crowned with three beautifully shaped domes covered with plates of pure gold. It was a perfect gem of art and beauty. But these plates of gold were removed after the siege and sold for prize money for the benefit of the army. [*Together, one presumes, with every available piece of gold used in decorative work or jewellery in the city of Delhi.* MMK]

Up to the time of the Mutiny, the King had entire control of and jurisdiction within the walls of the Palace; and any criminal or ruffian could secure an asylum there and could never be found if wanted. Hence it was really a den of thieves and murderers and criminals of all classes, a source of never-ending difficulty and annoyance to the British Government, and arrangements had been made to completely alter this state of things at the death of the King of Delhi. But the Mutiny did this for us, in that it cleared out this den of iniquity, as everyone fled from the Palace when our soldiers entered it, and thousands were killed.

Emerging from the Palace, there was a large open space planted with trees, as a great many of the old houses and streets had been destroyed in this quarter to improve the sanitary condition of the city, and thus a clear view was obtained of the Great Mosque, the Jumah Musjid, a most glorious building. Indeed, I think I know none in India to equal it. It stands on an eminence, whether natural or artificial I am not certain, and is approached on three sides by the most superb flights of steps, all of cut red sandstone, which lead from the level of the road up to the plateau on the top, the courtyard being entered through three magnificent red sandstone gateways, with galleries on the top.

As you enter at the principal gateway you find yourself within a superb courtyard capable of holding five thousand people at once, and at the further end rises a noble Mosque with three most beautiful domes of great size and graceful curves, made of white marble intersected with black lines. The courtyard too is paved with white marble panelled with lines of black, and the tall minarets which flank the mosque are a mixture of red sandstone and white and black marble. A beautiful wall of cut red sandstone surrounds the courtyard and unites the gateways to the mosque.

I have been up to one of the galleries in the Gateway to see the great crowd that assembles in that courtyard on the last day of the Great Mohammedan Fast, the Ramadan. On that occasion nearly five thousand people stood shoulder to shoulder in the courtyard in pure white dresses and turbans, and not a sound was to be heard save the voice of the officiating priest or Mullah who, standing in the mosque, sung out his address so that it could be heard at the furthest limit of the courtyard. When the call to prayer came, the whole of that vast crowd threw themselves on their knees and bowed their heads to the ground, as if they had been one man, and remained motionless until the prayer was ended.

It was a wonderful sight and a thrilling one, and when the crowd broke up and rushed out of the different gateways, no longer silent but jabbering at the pitch of their voices, another wonderful sight presented itself, for all these five thousand worshippers had left their leather shoes on the broad flights of steps outside the courtyard, and now they reclaimed them. It was always a puzzle to me how they could ever find their own footwear again, as the shoes lay side by side from the top to the bottom of the steps, and were almost all of the same pattern. 🗝

The Juma Masjid is today exactly as it was when Emily saw it. And as I did too, both as a child and later on when I was grown up and had children of my own. It still faces across the *maidan* – that large open space planted with trees that Emily describes – towards the enormous sandstone walls of the Red Fort and the Palace of Delhi; both mosque and fort seemingly unchanged by the three and a half centuries that have elapsed since Shahjehan, the self-styled "Ruler of the two Continents and Master of the two Seas", caused them to be built.

There are not many trees now, and far too many telegraph poles and electric light wires: but that is about all. Visitors can still climb up to the galleries on the top of the great main gateway, from where, on one of the Muslim festivals or on any Friday (the Mohammedan sabbath), they will see the self-same sight that Emily saw: hundreds of devout Muslims moving as one as they pray to Allah. But nowadays, I am afraid, the shoes will not be all of the same pattern, and too many of them will be in the European style. This may make it easier for the owners to recognize their own footwear, but lacks the charm of that sea of curl-toed shoes that once, but no longer, stood in endless rows upon every step of the vast sweep of red sandstone stairway that leads up to the entrance of the Emperor Shahjehan's great red and white mosque – originally named the "Masjid Jahannuma", but always known as the "Juma Masjid".

*T*here were numbers of other beautiful mosques in Delhi, and Jain temples. The latter beautiful buildings were of quite a different style of architecture to the Mohammedan mosque, but I never penetrated into a Jain temple until after the Mutiny, when in 1859 I went to Delhi and got the good incense that we still burn at Ascot.

Chandnee Chouk, which I have mentioned, was a narrow street, very picturesque indeed in its broken architecture, leading up to the Jumah Musjid, which was inhabited only by jewellers and silver-smiths. Of course they never displayed their wares in public, all their valuables being kept in boxes in the back rooms of the houses; the front room being open to the street, without doors, carpeted with a white cloth on which one or two men would be sitting, working at their trade, with some very simple tools and a small crucible alight for their metal work. If a European stopped at a shop he generally sat on the edge of the floor of the shop, which was always raised a few feet above the road, and bargained for any articles he wanted. I was never allowed to do this by my Father as he did not approve of English ladies entering any of these native shops.

But in January 1872, when we were at Delhi at the camp of exercise and Count Waldstein was with us, we made a large party of ladies and gentlemen and went to some of these shops, and those who could afford it got beautiful things, Mrs MacMurdo especially securing some rare specimens of crystal bowls. I had to be spokes-woman on these occasions, being able to speak the language better than most of the party. Once I begged the jeweller to show us any of the valuable jewellery worn by people in the Palace in the King's time, as I felt sure they must have got hold of some of the loot there, and he showed some beautiful articles which I had never before seen – bangles of turquoises, pearls, rubies, diamonds and emeralds, a dozen or so for each arm, shaped exactly like the silver bangles that we all possess.

One day while we were sitting at the edge of a shop examining these things a man from the outside crowd that surrounded our party thrust his arm over our heads and handed into the jeweller's shop a beautiful ankus that had belonged to the King of Delhi's mahout, the driver of his state elephant. This was a stick, about two feet long, of beautifully worked gold set with turquoises. The prong with which the mahout goaded the animal's head was made of the finest steel inlaid with gold and set with onyxes, and the knob at the end of the stick was superb cornelian, barred over with gold. Major Edward Burke, who was with us, immediately seized upon it, saying the Viceroy ought to have this regal weapon. He carried it off, telling the owner to come to the Viceroy's tent for payment. Ultimately, however, it became the property of Count Waldstein, who carried it off to Prague. ✣

One can only hope that the jeweller got paid for it. Emily does not say. I wonder where it is now and whether the Count's family still have it? or if it has come to rest in some museum or been blown to bits in a bombing raid during the last war? It is sad to think how many beautiful works of art must have been destroyed during and immediately after the Indian Mutiny, and, for that matter, during the First and Second World Wars – the golden treasures that Schliemann recovered from the ruins of Troy among them!

Anyone who wants to know what an "ankus", an elephant goad, looks like has only to turn to Rudyard Kipling's *Second Jungle Book*, where there is a drawing of one by his father, Lockwood Kipling, and a lovely story called "The King's Ankus".

*T*here was a fine building in Delhi in which the English Bank was established, but the house itself belonged to Dyce Sombre, who married Lord St Vincent's daughter, his great wealth weighing in the balance against his black blood. This house was inhabited by a family of the name of Beresford, the Father having charge of the bank, and I knew them well; the whole family was murdered on the day of the Mutiny, the bank looted, and the house in a great measure destroyed. But in the happy days of which I speak, no anxiety or fear of any such trouble ever entered anybody's mind, and we considered ourselves as safe there as if we were in London. 🙢

The Begum Sombre's house – the Bank House – was rebuilt, and was still a bank up to the day that the Raj ended in 1947. As far as I know, it still is, and the last time I saw it it did not look very different from the painting done of it for Sir Thomas' "Delhie Book" (see page 110). As for the Begum, she needs a book to herself, and I hear that one has recently been written: *All This Has Ended*, by Vera Chatterjee.

Her Highness the Begum was a fabulous character; a warrior princess of Hindustan who became the second wife of a German soldier-of-fortune named Walter Reinhardt. Walter rose to become a General in command of a mercenary army, and was known as "Sumroo" – the Indian version of a nickname bestowed upon him by his fellow Europeans on account of his dark complexion, "Le Sombre". After his death the Begum became converted to Christianity and, having taken over the leadership of his troops by popular acclaim, led them into battle. In her old age she adopted Sombre's great-grandson, Dyce, who inherited her vast fortune, and it was he who married one of Lord St Vincent's daughters. The semi-palace she built for herself in Delhi was leased to a bank, and partially destroyed on the day that the mutineers rode in from Meerut; the bank manager and his family (who lived in part of it) together with a great many of the loyal staff, being murdered by the mob.

Sir John Kaye, who wrote a contemporary account of the rising, says of the incident: "About noon the Delhi Bank was attacked and plundered, and all its chief servants, after a brave resistance, massacred. Mr Beresford, the manager of the Bank, took refuge with his wife and family on the roof of one of the outbuildings. And there, for some time, they stood at bay, he with a sword in his hand, ready to strike, while his courageous helpmate was armed with a spear. Thus, with resolute bravery, they defended the gorge of the staircase, until the assailants, seeing no hope of clearing the passage, retired to scale the walls in the rear of the house. The attack was then renewed, but still the little party on the roof made a gallant resistance. It is related by an eye-witness that one man fell dead beneath the lady's spear. But to resist was but to protract the pains of death. They were overpowered and killed, and the Bank was gutted from floor to roof."

Well, if he says so, it was. But either it was rebuilt to the same design or else the façade survived, because I can remember climbing those stairs when I went to the bank with my parents. In those days it stood in a little backwater, and could be reached only by a narrow alleyway between the shops that line the Chandni Chowk, Delhi's famous "Silver Street" – shops that presumably stand on what was once the Begum Sombre's front garden?

*T*here was also a great building called the Residency, where my uncle, Sir Charles Metcalfe, had lived when Resident at Delhi, somewhere between 1820 and 1839. This was used as a college for native gentlemen, and a very curious German, Dr Springer, was the Principal. His wife, also a worthy, but common, German whom I knew, told me she was obliged to hide her husband's evening trousers to prevent his going out of an evening and leaving her alone. 🙥

Here Emily's recollections come to an abrupt stop. It seems an odd place to end the accumulated memories of her long-ago youth in that golden period before the mine of the Mutiny exploded and the long rule of "John Company" came to a violent end. But at least she finishes on a light note – and Emily, as we know, liked to be "merry". All the same, one cannot help having a certain sympathy for both Dr Springer and his "worthy, but common" Frau. With him, because he was clearly a social-minded man who enjoyed the bright lights, but was either too poor to be able to afford a spare pair of evening trousers, or too timid to hide them before his wife got the chance to do so – or to call her bluff by going out in a day pair. And with her because she was obviously not included in many of the invitations to evening parties that came her husband's way (that unfortunate verdict "common" perhaps?) and was terrified of being left alone in this huge house in an alien land inhabited by dark-faced people who did not dress as she did, worshipped a variety of strange gods and godlings, ate peculiar food and spoke in a language that she did not understand!

Poor, worthy, frightened Frau Springer! We sympathize with you, and it is daunting to think how many wives of British and European men in the service of the East India Company must have felt as you did.

How fortunate were all those who, having been born in India, were always at home there – like Emily herself, whose own story does not stop here, thanks to the many letters and family papers lovingly preserved by the present owner of the delightful "Delhie Book", her great-grandson, Colonel John Ricketts. From these we learn that in 1848, the year following that joyous return to Delhi and her father's house, "dear Aunt Mary", while paying them a visit, asked if she might invite a young relative of her husband's to stay for a few days. The hospitable Sir Thomas having agreed, Edward Clive Bayley of the Bengal Civil Service arrived at Metcalfe House on a "very hot evening in July". He was twenty-seven and very shy. But although Emily (in a separate extant writing of hers) is reticent on the subject, it must clearly have been a case of love at first sight, because even as an old lady she can still clearly remember exactly what she was wearing when she met him for the first time at luncheon on the following day (and every woman knows what *that* means!): It was "An embroidered white muslin with three flounces and a blue sash", according to her recollection.

From then on, Edward seized every chance of visiting the Metcalfes in Delhi and making his number with Sir Thomas. But, although he seems to have confided his hopes to Aunt Mary, he was clearly a proper Victorian suitor, for he said nothing of his feelings to Emily until, in November 1849, he was offered the post of Under-Secretary in the Foreign Department – which meant that he would be stationed in Simla for at least three years, and able to provide a wife with a comfortable home in a good climate. Emily received his proposal by letter early in December but, since her father was away in camp and not expected back before Christmas, the betrothal was not announced until the 3rd of February 1850.

She married Edward in March, in Colonel Skinner's church, St James's, near Delhi's Kashmir Gate, and after a honeymoon spent at Dil-Koosha, the Metcalfes' house at the Kutub, travelled up to Simla to live with her husband at a house that is still there and that many "Simla-ites" besides myself will remember well, "The Priory".

The Governor-General, Lord Dalhousie, and his wife were very kind to Emily and Edward, and took the newly-weds on a long trek through the Simla hills. Emily gives a lyrical description of the hill country beyond Simla, every word of which could be applied to it with equal truth today, since to my mind it remains one of the most enchanting places in the world. Those who would like a really good description of it as it was then – and still is – have only to turn to Rudyard Kipling's *Second Jungle Book* and read the story entitled "The Miracle of Puran Bhagat". The hero of that haunting tale, a one-time "Prime Minister of no small state", took that very road. And the road, as Puran Bhagat saw it, and as Emily and Edward saw it, and as I and thousands of others have seen it, will have changed very little – if at all. Every turn and twist in it, and every breathtaking view, will still be there, waiting to catch at the traveller's heart.

Towards the end of this trip Emily became unwell, and by October, when they returned to Simla and "The Priory", she was in such poor health that a certain Dr Hay reported her to be "very ill" – too ill to remain in India: she was to be sent home to England as early as possible. In spite of her grief and dismay at the prospect of being parted from Edward, a passage was booked for her on a ship sailing from Calcutta in the second week of December. Her luggage had already been packed and sent on ahead, when, she writes, on the very night that she herself was due to leave Simla, "we were startled by the birth of our first child!"

Apparently it had never occurred to anyone that there might be a perfectly ordinary explanation for her "illness" – least of all to Emily. One wonders if she still believed in the gooseberry-bush theory? Her own mother had been dead for many years, and possibly Aunt Mary had jibbed at telling her young niece the facts of life. All the same, Edward must have been pretty dim not to have noticed anything odd, and he cannot have improved matters by fainting when "the doctor told him of the event that had taken place".

When he finally came to, the joyful father rushed out to see if he could get any clothing for his newly born daughter, since none had been provided. He returned with an "exquisitely embroidered French cambric robe and a pink plush cloak!!" – the double exclamation marks are

Emily's, and no wonder. (No diapers, you notice, although there must have been dish-cloths available.)

The passage to England was cancelled and after that there was no more talk of ill health.

Their next posting was to the Kangra Valley, which is another enchantingly beautiful spot, and here they lived for several happy years. But down in the plains, at Delhi, all was not so well.

Bahadur Shah the Moghul still styled himself "King of Delhi", and his palace, and the Red Fort in which it was built, remained under his royal sway; although, apart from this, he wielded little or no power – that having passed into the hands of the East India Company. Yet the fact that he ruled over the Red Fort meant that anyone taking sanctuary there was under his personal protection and safe from British law or justice; with the not unnatural result that, as Emily has noted, the whole vast complex was crammed with murderers, thieves, kidnappers and other criminals, who thumbed their noses at authority and lived safely in his shadow.

The Governor-General, together with the Directors of the East India Company, had decided long ago that this mediaeval nonsense must now cease, and that as soon as the present Moghul died the title of "King of Delhi" must die with him. To this end there had been protracted negotiations with the Heir Apparent, who was eventually persuaded to agree to this on condition that he retained his right to live in the palace and draw his full stipend as King, which would enable him to feed, clothe and house not only himself but all the members of the royal family, as befitted their rank.

Bahadur Shah himself showed little interest in the negotiations, considering that they did not concern him, since had not the Court astrologer predicted that he would be the last of the Moghuls and that after him there would be no other? But his wife the Queen would not be persuaded. Zeenut Mahal had always hated the British, and now she raved and threatened, and swore that she would be revenged upon all who had planned this thing – they should die by poison, every one!

Sir Thomas Metcalfe, as Resident of Delhi, had naturally taken part in the negotiations, and when in November of 1853, at the age of 58, he died from an unknown cause it was assumed by all that he had been poisoned on the orders of Zeenut Mahal. Emily certainly believed it and she was probably right. India has always known a great deal about vegetable poisons that are not easy to trace, and, in a country where the climate ensures that a body must be buried or burned within a few hours of death, an autopsy – particularly in those days – was a waste of time. Theo's wife also was to die in a mysterious manner, and who can say that poison did not play a part in that too?

But it would not be long before Zeenut Mahal would have the chance to revenge herself on many more of the British, and when, three and a half years after Sir Thomas' death, the Mutiny broke out she seized it with both hands and drove her reluctant old husband into supporting the mutineers and later murdering those wretched survivors of the first day's massacre who had been imprisoned in the palace.

Emily was fortunate enough to miss the Mutiny, since she and Edward and their children sailed for England in May 1857 – the very month in which it broke out. But apart from an occasional spell of "home leave" she was to spend the best part of the next thirty years and more in India. She left the country with her husband (by now Sir Edward) on his retirement in 1878 and, when he died six years later, lived on into the present century and the reign of George V.

One cannot say of her that she married "and lived happily ever after", because she must have had her share of sorrow. She lost two of the thirteen children she bore her "beloved Edward" – a daughter born in Calcutta in 1863 and a son born in Simla in 1869 (although in this she was luckier than most, since in India the average for those days was two out of every five). She barely knew her mother, had to see her greatly loved father die of poison, and was a widow for more than a quarter of a century. But there were compensations: many of them. The same that India gives all who live there.

Unimaginable beauty. The chance to wake at dawn and see from one's window the long line of the Himalayas spanning the horizon, and to watch the peaks catch fire, one after another, as the sun comes up. To see the enormous stretch of the plains at evening, when the smoke from the cooking fires draws out like long blue veils and the cattle come straggling back from the grazing grounds, and every canebrake is full of fireflies. To watch the enormous Indian moon lift slowly up through the dusty green twilight to glimmer on marble domes and minarets and carved temples that were old when Elizabeth I was young. To stroll through the clamour and the colour of the bazaars, listen to sitars and tom-toms, and to smell the scent of jasmine and frangi-pani and water on hot, dry ground.

We who were born to all this, and lived in India and loved her, can truthfully say that our lives were indeed "fallen unto us in pleasant places".

Index

Page numbers in roman type refer to the text, those in **bold** to the pages from Sir Thomas Metcalfe's "Delhie Book". Both Emily, Lady Clive Bayley, and Sir Thomas Metcalfe used various spellings for Indian names: where two versions of the same name differ greatly, the versions are indexed separately; otherwise the commonest form is given.

Acknowledgements

The Publishers would like to thank all those who, through their interest, patience and considerable help, have made possible the publication of this book. In particular they would like to thank Mildred Archer, Ursula Sims-Williams and B.C. Bloomfield, of the India Office Library; Mrs Eric Theophilus Metcalfe and her daughter, Miss Peggy Metcalfe; and Miss Felicité Hardcastle. J. Talboys Wheeler's The History of the Imperial Assemblage at Delhi (1877) was an important source used in the compilation of the Introduction.

سلطانی

شاه جهان آباد

سایر و مال علاقة دار الخلافة

اکبر آباد بهادر و صاحب کمشنر بهادر کمپنی

نوبر جنرل بهادر مختار امور سرکار دولت ممالک

جان طامس سافلس متنفذ بهادر فیره و نجابت صارم

فم لیل احمد له معظم الدوله امین الملک الخصال

عقیدت اختصاص صلاح یق العنایت ولا

امارت و ایالت هم

حاصل

فیلی